AN ILLUSTRATED
GUIDEBOOK TO CRACOW

JAN ADAMCZEWSKI

AN ILLUSTRATED GUIDEBOOK

TO CRACOW

INTERPRESS PUBLISHERS

Translated by Bogan Piotrowska
Designed by Stanisław Szczuka
Production editor: Wiesław Pyszka
Maps by Wojciech Szczawiński and Andrzej Bujarski
Photographs by A. Bujak, Z. Łagocki, S. Markowski, S. Michta, J. Podlecki
and K. K. Pollesch
Photograph on the cover by Z. Łagocki
This publication appears also in Polish, French, German and Russian
This is the two thousand four hundred and twenty-fourth publication
of Interpress
Set, printed and bound in Czechoslovakia
ISBN 83-223-2424-3

List of maps and plans

Cracow   6

The Royal Tract   18

Wawel   54

Museums   92

Higher Education Institutions   120

Wit Stwosz's Marian Altar   130

Kazimierz   138

Nowa Huta   160

Cracow Districts   170

TABLE OF CONTENTS

INTRODUCTION _____ 9

THE ROYAL TRACT _____ 19

WAWEL HILL _____ 55

MUSEUMS _____ 93

THE COLLEGIUM MAIUS
AND THE UNIVERSITY QUARTER ___ 121

WIT STWOSZ
AND ST. MARY'S CHURCH _____ 131

KAZIMIERZ _____ 139

CRACOW DISTRICTS _____ 149

NOWA HUTA _____ 161

ENVIRONS _____ 169

PRACTICAL INFORMATION _____ 187

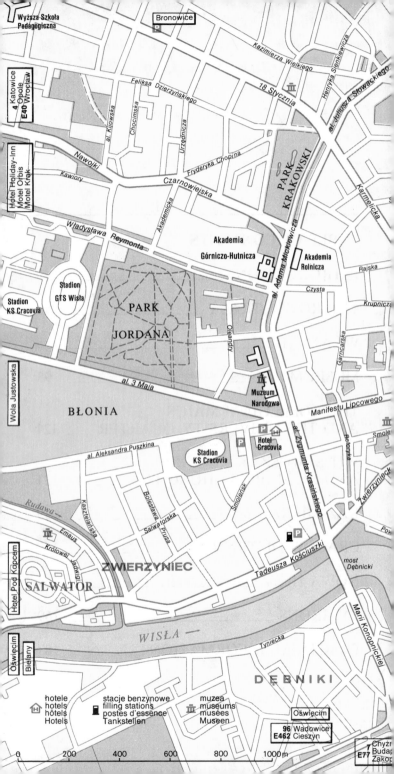

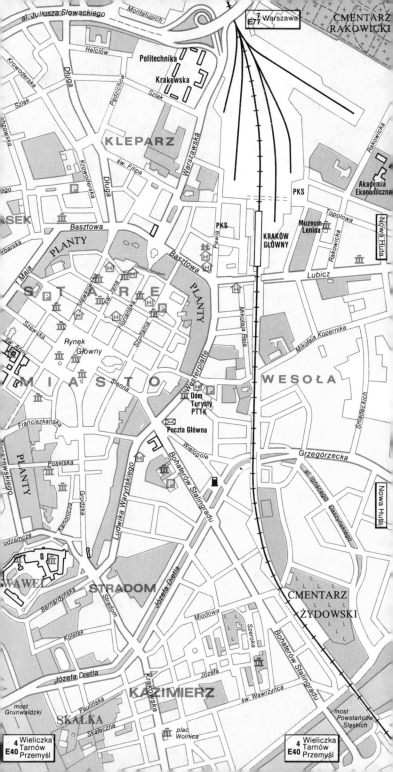

North-western view of Cracow in 1603—05, in *Theatri . . . mundi urbium liber sextus* by J. Braun and A. Hoghenberg, Cologne 1618

INTRODUCTION

Cracovia totius Poloniae urbs celeberrima atque amplissima, regia atque Academia insignis — Cracow, the most famous and glorious town in all of Poland, distinguished by virtue of its royal residence and the Academy. This inscription was emblazoned in 1619 by the etcher Matthäus Merian on his copperplate, known as the Amsterdam print, which shows a vast panorama of contemporary Cracow, over two metres long. Cracow had had to work long to earn such a verdict which has been valid for many centuries and is still true today. For no other town in Poland can boast such a large number of historic monuments and none has continued as a symbol of Polish tradition and culture for such a long time. Although repeatedly looted and destroyed by fires and wars, it always rose from the ruins and returned to its former splendour.

Within its present boundaries, Cracow has some 6,000 historic buildings and monuments, as many as 4,000 of them in the city centre. These include over 5,500 residential buildings, 140 ecclesiastical edifices, 60 defensive and fortification constructions, 51 public utility buildings, 74 residences, mansions and manor houses, and 118 parks and gardens. At the same time Cracow possesses Poland's largest collection of works of art, estimated at about 2.3 million items, including 1.6 million in Cracow museums and some 700,000 items in churches, monasteries and private collections.

Small wonder then that, acting on its convention on the international protection of monuments of nature and culture, the UNESCO World Heritage Committee session held in Washington, D.C., in September 1978, placed the architectural and historic complex of Cracow, together with the nearby salt mine of Wieliczka, on the list of the first twelve major historic sites in the world.

Unfortunately owing to the inexorable passing of time, and the numerous disasters that befell the city, many of its historic monuments are in a bad state of repair. In order to prevent the complete destruction of the Old Town a large-scale campaign has been undertaken to rescue the most valuable sites from further destruction. In 1978 a Civic Committee for the Reconstruction of Cracow's Historic Architecture was set up, and in 1986 the Seym (parliament) adopted a special resolution on the protection of the city's monuments. Donations in support of this cause are flowing in from all over Poland and from Poles living abroad. The entire project is on a scale never hitherto seen in Poland. The painstaking and time-consuming operation is performed on the live organism of the city that continues as usual following its daily routine amidst all the bustle caused by the restoration effort.

In the course of conservation work many discoveries have been made and our knowledge of the history of Cracow has been widened. For example, in an annex of the Chapter House (13 Kanonicza Street) a 9th century ducal treasure trove was unearthed, containing iron axes (pre-monetary items of tender) weighing almost four tons.

A ducal treasure trove dating from the 9th century? How old, then, is Cracow? It is not easy to answer this question for according to the archaeologists this area has been settled for 50,000 years and in the vicinity, in the Ojców caves, traces of human habitation date from 200,000 years ago.

And what do the written sources say? The learned traveller Ibrahim ibn-Jacob, who in 965/966 as a physician and translator accompanied the mission of the Caliph of Cordova to the Emperor Otto I (962—973), mentioned Cracow in his account as an important commercial centre. In the year 1000 the bishopric of Cracow was established and in 1038 Cracow became the capital of the country. The city developed rapidly and Romanesque Cracow, with its castle at Wawel Hill and over twenty churches, did not differ much from the other central and western European capitals.

Following destruction wrought by Tatar invasions, of which two in particular, in 1241 and 1242, brought in their wake tremendous losses, the then ruler, Prince Boleslaus the

Bashful, had to carry out thorough repair and in fact to build and fortify the city virtually anew. This is the origin of the final location of the city according to Magdeburg law in 1257. The mediaeval town-planners laid out a huge square (200 by 200 metres) with streets running from it perpendicularly. This chessboard arrangement, preserved until today, is interrupted by some Romanesque buildings dating from before 1257 which are oriented and in relation to the general layout situated at an angle. All structures built after that date in Gothic style stand along the streets laid out at the time.

In the 13th—15th centuries Gothic Cracow acquired many magnificent churches, a Cloth Hall, a Town Hall, burgher houses and walls with gates and towers; and Okół, a settlement that had separated Cracow from Wawel, was incorporated in the city. Two new neighbouring towns were established, Kazimierz in 1335 and Kleparz in 1366. In his *Chronicle*, Marcin Bielski, an outstanding 16th century historian, compared Cracow to a lute or an eagle: "It has something of an Eagle with Wawel representing its head and Grodzka Street being its neck, while the suburbs around it are like some kind of wings."

In 1364 King Casimir the Great founded a university. The state that was developing quickly needed an efficient administration, educated officers and enlightened teachers to set up a vast network of schools. The university grew rapidly and was given a new lease of life during the reign of Queen Jadwiga and King Ladislaus Jagiello whose name — the Jagiellonian University — it bears. The importance and fame of the Cracow academy went beyond the Polish borders. During the period when Nicolaus Copernicus (1491—95) was one of its students, it was attended by young people from almost all of Europe.

In 1493 the German geographer Hartmann Schedel noted in his *Weltchronik:* "Cracow has a famous university, rich in many excellent and highly learned men, where numerous liberal arts are taught."

The importance of Cracow resulted not only from its political role as the capital of the country and a significant centre of learning, but also from the rulers' concern about the development of art and culture. Consequently Cracow attracted many outstanding scholars and artists greedy for fame and money and for a possibility of artistic fulfilment, the best example being Veit Stoss (Wit Stwosz), a wood carver from Nuremberg, who produced his major works in Cracow, for example the famous altar-piece in St. Mary's Church, the attractive epitaph of Kallimach in the Dominican church and the sarcophagus of Casimir the Jagiellon in Wawel Cathedral.

The 16th century — known as the Golden Age — meant for Poland and for Cracow in particular a period of exceptional development. The new current in art, called the Renaissance, brought a period when science, learning and art flourished in Cracow. The new structures built at that time followed new Italian models. The entire royal residence on Wawel Hill was enlarged and thoroughly rebuilt in the course of almost thirty years. In 1518 Cracow gave a warm welcome to the Italian princess Bona Sforza, wife of King Sigismund I. At that time the capital of the powerful Jagiellon state had 30,000 inhabitants, trade and crafts developed and there were as many as sixty guilds in the city. Excellent Italian architects and sculptors — including Francesco Fiorentino, Bartolommeo Berrecci, Gianmaria Padovano and Santi Gucci — gave the town a new image and their art had a considerable impact on local artists. After the first Polish postal service connected Cracow with Italy in 1558 it took only three and a half days for a letter to reach Vienna.

With the death of Sigismund II Augustus, the last of the Jagiellon kings, in 1572, the era of Cracow's peaceful development came to an end. In any case, following the union with the Grand Duchy of Lithuania (real union in 1569), Cracow found itself on the remote outskirts of an enormous state. Seym sessions and elections of new monarchs took place in Warsaw which was more centrally situated. King Sigismund III Vasa (1587—1632), who was at the same time king of Sweden and wanted to be closer to his native country, took advantage of the fire that in 1595 ravaged Wawel to move to Warsaw together with his court. On 25 May 1609 the monarch left Wawel for good and the capital of Poland was transferred to Warsaw, though without any formal legal act.

Despite the transfer of the royal residence to Warsaw, Cracow cathedral continued to be the place of coronation and burial site of Polish kings. It was also customarily the site of royal ingresses on the occasion of weddings or victories on the field of battle.

The period of the Counter-Reformation left a special imprint on Cracow. Instead of the royal court, it was the court of the Cracow bishops that came to the fore. New monastic orders arrived in Cracow and built their own churches and monasteries of which there were over fifty. The calm forms of Renaissance architecture were replaced with Mannerist and Baroque elements. However the former glory was a thing of the past. The city felt painfully the absence of the royal court. "Since you, Your Royal Highness, left this town, not an acre has been added to it," Jerzy Zborowski told King Sigismund III in 1627 when the latter asked him about matters in Cracow. Besides, the 17th century was a period of upheavals in Poland and therefore in Cracow too. In 1655 for the first time in its history, Cracow was captured and looted by the Swedes following a long siege. Decline of trade, crafts, art and learning set in.

Throughout the 18th century Cracow was repeatedly besieged, captured and plundered by Swedish, Russian, Austrian and Prussian armies. In 1787 its population, together with the suburbs, was less than 10,000. The condition of Wawel was so appalling that Stanislaus Augustus (Poniatowski), the last king of Poland, was given permission by the Seym to be crowned in Warsaw instead of Cracow.

During the years of the country's greatest decline and later during the partition period Cracow became a centre of national liberation movements. On 24 March 1794 Thaddeus Kosciuszko proclaimed a national insurrection and in the Cracow Market Place swore that he would use the authority entrusted to him in the cause of independent Poland and general freedom. However Kosciuszko's rebellion was defeated and Cracow was occupied by the Prussians who in October 1795 took the Wawel royal insignia to Berlin where the gold was melted down and made into coins, and the priceless jewels that had adorned the crowns were torn out and sold. Only the Szczerbiec

(Jagged Sword), the coronation sword, survived and years later returned to Wawel where it is now the gem of the royal treasury.

Following the third partition of Poland, Cracow was occupied by Austria. This first occupation of Cracow began in 1795 and ended in 1809 when troops of the Duchy of Warsaw formed by Napoleon entered the city. In 1809—15 Cracow was the capital of one of the *départements* in the Duchy of Warsaw and between 1815 and 1846 the capital of the Republic of Cracow, a diminutive piece of unoccupied Poland 1164 sq. km. in area, established by the decision of the Congress of Vienna. Although the three invaders, Austria, Russia and Prussia, exercised close supervision over the Republic, they could not prevent the development of secret national movements. In 1846 the Cracow Revolution, a harbinger of the wave of revolutionary upheavals in Europe in 1848, promised to annul differences between the estates and land to landless peasants. The revolution failed however, its leader, Edward Dembowski, was killed and foreign troops entered Cracow. The Republic was abolished and together with Cracow incorporated into Austria, which held the town until 1918.

In the early 19th century, following the example of many western cities, the mediaeval walls were pulled down, with the exception of a small section near the Florian Gate and the Barbican. The same fate befell the Gothic town hall and the municipal granary. In place of the old walls, the Planty park was laid out round the Old Town. Cracow began to expand beyond the city walls and new districts came into being. In 1850 a great fire destroyed almost half of the old town centre.

On receiving autonomous status in 1866 Cracow became a major centre of Polish learning, art and culture that served national history and tradition. In 1872, the Cracow Learned Society, which was founded in 1816, was transformed into the Academy of Learning, and during the period of national servitude this was the only organization representing Polish science and learning.

The second half of the 19th century saw the beginnings of modern industry and the development of the labour movement and socialist ideology. In 1880 Cracow witnessed the trial of 35 socialist leaders, including Ludwik Waryński, the founder of the First Proletariat, the first Polish workers' party. In 1894 the first major strike took place here. In 1902 Feliks Dzierżyński ran in Cracow a publishing press of the Social-Democratic Party of the Kingdom of Poland and Lithuania and Ignacy Daszyński, a socialist leader, was active here. In 1912—14 Lenin lived in Cracow and until the outbreak of the First World War directed from here the revolutionary movement inside Russia.

In the late 19th and early 20th centuries a Polish artistic avantgarde was born in Cracow and loosed a veritable revolution against the old currents in art. This new artistic and literary movement was known as Young Poland. Cracow's Academy of Fine Arts employed some of the best Polish artists, including Julian Fałat, Leon Wyczółkowski, Jacek Malczewski, Jan Stanisławski, Stanisław Wyspiański and Józef Mehoffer, and helped spread new artistic ideas to the rest of the country.

Well-known painters, poets, musicians and authors established what became the first and most famous Polish literary cabaret, the "Green Balloon", in the renowned "Jama Michalikowa" café, which is still in existence in 45 Floriańska Street. It was an extravagant, crazy cabaret and for its founders, who both wrote texts and performed in it, nothing was sacred in the old, venerable Cracow.

The hope of an armed conflict between the partitioning powers — Austria and Prussia on the one hand and Russia on the other — intensified national liberation movements in Cracow where in fact all Polish political parties operated, some of them illegally. In 1910 the paramilitary "Strzelec" (Rifleman) association came into being and subsequently many rifle detachments were formed. The provisional commission of the confederated independence parties, established in Vienna in 1912, had its headquarters in Cracow where its leaders, Ignacy Daszyński and Józef Piłsudski, lived at the time. Finally it was from Cracow, from Oleandry near Błonia, that on 6 August 1914 Piłsudski led the first rifle company of the famous Polish Legions to the Kingdom of Poland.

The defeat of the partitioning powers in 1918 brought Poland freedom and Cracow again became an important administrative, academic, cultural, and industrial centre. In 1919 it acquired a new higher education institution, the Academy of Mining (today the Academy of Mining and Metallurgy).

During the Second World War in 1939—45 the Nazis turned Cracow into the capital of the so-called Government General and proceeded to destroy everything that was Polish; higher education institutions, secondary schools, theatres and museums all were closed down. On 6 November 1939, 183 professors of the Jagiellonian University and the Academy of Mining were deported to concentration camps. The Jewish population was murdered. Works of art, including Wit Stwosz's altar-piece, were taken to the Reich. In spite of the mortal danger involved, despite the threat of forced labour in Germany and deportation to concentration camps, execution and imprisonment, Cracow did not give in; it continued its fight. Over 800 students attended secret university courses; conspiratorial secondary schools operated; a large-scale underground movement carried out numerous armed and sabotage actions.

On 18 January 1945 Cracow was liberated by the Soviet Army. A new epoch began for the city. Cracow, which in 1939 had 260,000 inhabitants, expanded to more than 800,000 (1,200,000 in the entire agglomeration), and after Warsaw and Łódź, is Poland's third largest city.

Not without reason the Jagiellonian University is referred to as the Polish Alma Mater; since the last war many of its faculties have been turned into autonomous institutions. Cracow is the home of 14 theatres of which three — the Juliusz Słowacki, Stary and Cricot 2 — are among Poland's leading theatre companies. Besides, there are numerous cabarets (including the celebrated "Piwnica pod Baranami"), student companies, amateur and workers' groups.

Cracow plays host to many national and international artistic events which attract crowds of tourists. These include the Days of Organ Music (spring), the Student Theatre Reminiscences (March), the Student Song Festival (May), the National and International Short-film Festivals (late May and early June), the Art Festival (June), the Music in Old Cracow Festival (August), and the Folk Art Fair (September), all held annually. There are also the

Architectural Biennale (the first of which took place in 1985), the International Graphic Art Biennale (in even years), the Animated Film Festival (every four years in October) and the Wanda Landowska Harpsichord Competition (every eight years).

Cracow carries out cooperation and cultural exchanges with many of its twin-cities in various parts of the world, for example with Bologna and Florence in Italy, Bordeaux in France, Liège in Belgium, Nuremberg in West Germany, Rochester, N.Y., in the United States, Kiev in the USSR, Leipzig in East Germany, Bratislava in Czechoslovakia, Turnovo in Bulgaria, Zagreb in Yugoslavia and Fès in Morocco.

In 1978 the archbishop of Cracow, Karol Cardinal Wojtyła, was elected the 264th successor of Saint Peter in Rome. He took the name of John Paul II and is the first non-Italian Pope in 455 years. He was born in the small town of Wadowice near Cracow and during the Second World War was a worker in the stone quarry of the "Solvay" chemical plant in Cracow.

Modern Cracow also means large-scale industry which places the city among Poland's leading industrial centres. The socialized sector of the economy employs 370,000. The year 1950 saw the beginning of the construction of a large metallurgical combine which was given the name of the Lenin Steel Mill in 1954. Within its administrative boundaries there are also new chemical, pharmaceutical and other plants. Cracow manufactures 58 per cent of Poland's iron, 45 per cent of steel, 42 per cent of cigarettes, and 27 per cent of medicines. Unfortunately, industrial pollution damages the walls of the venerable churches and houses and is harmful to the natural environment of the Cracow agglomeration which has a population of over one million.

However it is not that modern Cracow of industry and new housing developments that each year draws millions of tourists. They are lured here by the beauty of the old architecture, the magnificent museums with their numerous works of art, old narrow streets and lanes, ancient churches and monasteries crammed with treasures of art and by that unique, atmosphere of history and the mood of the old Polish tradition to which every new arrival succumbs.

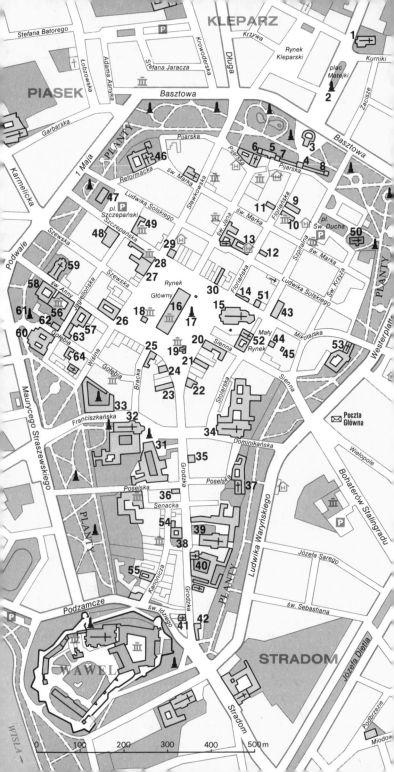

THE ROYAL TRACT

Cracow's major tourist route is the Royal Tract boasting the city's most magnificent churches, mansions and monuments and encompassing busy shopping streets and quiet lanes: that is, everything that makes this thousand year old town so attractive.

The Royal Tract begins at JANA MATEJKI SQUARE with the Grunwald monument in its centre. However let us first have a look at the **Church of St. Florian** (1) which stands slightly to one side. Its origins are associated with Prince Casimir (II) the Just (1177—94) who, on ascending

---

1. St. Florian's Church; 2. Grunwald Memorial; 3. Barbican; 4. Florian Gate; 5. Municipal Arsenal; 6. Carpenters' Tower; 7. Joiners' and Rope-makers' Tower; 8. Haberdashers' Tower; **Floriańska Street:** 9. no. 45 ("Jama Michalikowa" café); 10. no. 41 (Jan Matejko Museum); 11. Under the Bells House at no. 24; 12. no. 17; 13. no. 14 (Under the Rose Hotel); 14. Under the Negroes House; **Main Market Place :** 15. St. Mary's Church; 16. Cloth Hall; 17. Adam Mickiewicz statue; 18. Town Hall Tower; 19. St. Adalbert's Church; 20. Grey House at no. 6; 21. no. 9; 22. Under the Gold Head House at no. 13; 23. Under St. Anne House at no. 14; 24. Hetmans' House; 25. Jabłonowski Mansion; 26. Under the Rams Mansion; 27. Spis Mansion at no. 34; 28. Krzysztofory Mansion at no. 35; 29. Under the Stag House at no. 36; 30. Under the Eagle House at no. 47; 31. Wielopolski Mansion; 32. Franciscan church and monastery; 33. Bishops' Palace; 34. Dominican church and monastery; **Grodzka Street:** 35. no. 32; 36. no. 39; 37. St. Joseph's Church and Bernardine convent; 38. Collegium Iuridicum; 39. Church of St. Peter and St. Paul; 40. St. Andrew's Church; 41. St. Giles' Church; 42. Royal Arsenal; 43. City Centre Community Club in the Lamelli Mansion; 44. Szober House; 45. Residential Tower; 46. Church and monastery of the Reformati; 47. Palace of Art; 48. Stary (Old) Theatre; 49. Szołayski House; 50. Holy Cross Church; **Mariacki Square:** 51. Hippolitów House at no. 3; 52. St. Barbara's Church; 53. Church of Our Lady of the Snows; **Kanonicza Street:** 54. no. 6 (Society of the Friends of the Fine Arts); 55. Chapter House; 56. Collegium Maius; 57. Kołłątaj College; 58. Nowodworski College; 59. St. Anne's Church; 60. Collegium Novum; 61. Copernicus statue; 62. Collegium Minus; 63. Collegium Physicum; 64. Collegium Slavisticum

the throne in Cracow, discovered that the town — at that time already an important urban centre — had no holy relics. Therefore the pope gave Cracow the remains of St. Florian, a Roman knight and martyr who had lived during the period of the Emperor Diocletian. Legend has it that when in 1184 the procession carrying the relics was approaching the town, and the prince, the clergy and Cracow inhabitants went forward to greet it, the ashes of the saint suddenly grew so heavy that the bearers were unable to move forward. This was seen as a sign from heaven and to commemorate the event a church dedicated to Saint Florian was built on the spot.

Since then whenever a Polish king died outside Cracow, his body was carried in a solemn procession to Wawel where it was buried in the cathedral crypt. Before that, however, the ashes used to be deposited in St. Florian's Church which was where the funeral cortège started for Wawel. Similarly when a newly elected king arrived in Cracow for the coronation, the joyous procession also began in St. Florian's Church.

The modest Church of St. Florian — six times restored following wars and fires since its situation outside the city walls made it an easy prey — gave its name to Cracow's most beautiful gate and busiest street (Floriańska). First however let us take a look at the **Grunwald Memorial** (2) showing King Ladislaus Jagiello (1386—1434) who in 1410 defeated the Knights of the Teutonic Order in the battle of Grunwald. This monument was endowed in 1910 by the famous Polish musician and statesman, Ignacy Jan Paderewski. Destroyed by the Nazis immediately on their entering the city, it was restored in 1976. Next to it you can see the symbolic **Tomb of the Unknown Soldier,** the place of official celebrations, where on the anniversaries of the liberation of Poland and Cracow, flowers are laid by the town's inhabitants.

The area of the Grunwald Memorial commands a view of the Old Town, its walls, the Barbican and towers which formed a protection against the enemies, admittedly not always effective. Not much has been left of the walls that once encircled the entire city, the construction of which began in the 13th and ended in the 15th centuries. What has survived are the **Barbican** (3), its present form going back to the years 1498—99, which is considered the largest structure of this kind in Europe; the beautiful **Florian Gate** (4) dating from 1300; the Renaissance **Municipal Arsenal** (5); the **Carpenters'** (6), **Joiners' and Rope-makers'** (7) and **Haberdashers'** (8) **Towers,** and the bits of wall that connect them. In summer the Barbican is the site of various open-air events. The Arsenal houses part of the Czartoryski Collections (a branch of the National Museum) and the stone walls serve as an art gallery for students of the Academy of Fine Arts and amateur artists.

The Planty, a belt of attractive shady promenades encircling the Old Town, was laid out over 160 years ago in place of the dismantled fortifications and moats.

This street of several hundred metres in length, known from time immemorial as FLORIAŃSKA, at the end of which stands the monumental mass of St. Mary's Church, was laid out in 1257, in the final location plan of Cracow. The houses along the street, originally Gothic in style, in time became converted to Renaissance, Baroque or neo-Classicism. Conservation operations that here have proceeded with particular intensity have resulted in the discovery of old façades and interiors and restored their former splendour to ancient portals, window stonework and emblems which in the days of yore served instead of house numbers and signboards of shops.

Proceeding in the direction of the Main Market Place we pass **house no. 45** (9) with its famous "Jama Michalikowa" café which in the early 20th century played host to the "Green Balloon" cabaret the traditions of which are today continued by the "Jama Michalikowa" cabaret. The Baroque **house at no. 41** is the family home of, and today the museum devoted to Jan Matejko (10), the famous painter of monumental historical scenes who lived and worked here between 1873 and 1893. The museum has a rich collection of mementos of the famous artist and is at the same time an example of a well-preserved interior of a burgher house. **No. 24** (11), known as Podedzwony (Under the Bells) bears a fine emblem in the form of three bells since for many centuries it used to be the home and workshop of one of the Cracow bell founders. The corner **house at no. 17** (12) is hung with old chains of which only a few have survived to our times. In days of yore, during sieges and internal tumults such chains were used to bar the streets in order to protect the city's inhabitants. The **Hotel pod Różą** (Under the Rose) at no. 14 (13) is one of the oldest hotels in Cracow and its celebrated visitors included Franz Liszt and Tsar Alexander I (though, in spite of what the commemorative tablet on its wall says, not Balzac — who during his stay in Cracow stopped at the Hotel Under a White Rose at Stradom). The handsome Gothic cellars of the hotel have been turned into a popular cabaret and a children's theatre, Drops. The last house on the left side is the **Under the Negroes House** (14) (the first floor façade is adorned with a 16th century bas-relief representation of two Negroes); it once held a famous pharmacy also selling excellent wine.

And thus we reached the MAIN MARKET PLACE (Rynek Główny), the oldest and most beautiful of Cracow's squares. When in 1257 Duke Boleslaus the Bashful signed the city's location charter it surely did not cross his mind that the square measuring 200 by 200 metres would for centuries serve the town as its focal point. Together with St. Mark's Square in Venice, the Main Market Place in Cracow is considered one of the most magnificent town-planning projects in the world.

In the past the Market Place was densely built up; it had a Gothic town hall with a tower, a Renaissance granary, a large weigh-house, a foundry, stalls, a pillory and a Cloth Hall. Of these only the monumental building of the Cloth Hall, the small Church of St. Adalbert and the lonely Town Hall Tower, have been left.

Centuries ago inhabitants of the old capital of Poland gathered in the Market Place to attend various state ceremonies. In 1525, by Bracka Street (today, the place is marked by a commemorative tablet with its inscription saying "The Prussian Homage 1525"), Albrecht Hohenzol-

Statue of King Ladislaus Jagiello, endowed in 1910 by the famous Polish pianist and composer Ignacy Jan Paderewski, on the occasion of the 500th anniversary of the victorious battle fought at Grunwald in 1410 against the Order of Teutonic Knights. Designed by Antoni Wiwulski and Franciszek Black. Destroyed by the Germans in 1939, restored in 1976

Late 15th century Barbican which protected the city from the east. Built of brick on a circular plan 24.4 metres in diameter, with its walls over three metres thick. It has 130 loop-holes in four rows

lern, the last grand master of the Teutonic Order defeated by Poland, paid homage to King Sigismund (I) the Old, by which act the Prussian state originated.

On the same spot, beginning in 1320, the Polish kings, on the day following the coronation, received homage from the burghers who handed the monarch the golden key to the city gates and 1000 ducats. Cracow paid tribute to the king in the name of all Polish towns and the king confirmed the privileges of the burghers.

The national insurrection against tsarist Russia began in the Market Place on 24 March 1794, where Thaddeus Kosciuszko took an oath to the nation and proclaimed an "Act of Insurrection of the citizens, inhabitants of the Cracow voivodship". The place where Kosciuszko made his vows, between the Town Hall Tower and Szewska Street, is also marked with a special plaque beside which Poles lay flowers on the anniversary of the rebellion. Next to it there is a huge money-box where Cracovians and tourists drop money to help towards the conservation of Cracow's monuments.

It was in the Market Place that the notorious wizard Pan Twardowski frolicked, breaking the clay pots of the sellers; where Stańczyk, the most famous royal jester in Polish history, sauntered among the strollers and poked fun at the Cracow burghers; where ceremonious parades and meetings as well as public executions took place. Today, too, more important public ceremonies are held in the Market Place over which hundreds of pigeons fly. These are not just ordinary pigeons, in fact, but the knights of Duke Henry (IV) Probus (from 1288 prince of Cracow) who according to legend were cursed and turned into pigeons.

Planty, a municipal park over 50 acres in area encircling the Old Town, laid out in the early 19th century in place of the two dismantled lines of walls and moats

For the past 600 years, with short breaks, from the higher tower of **St. Mary's Church** (15) a bugle call has been sounded every hour to be heard all over the town. It is associated with another legend from the times of Tatar invasions. When the trumpeter on top of the tower saw the approaching enemy he sounded the alarm for the city. Unfortunately he did not manage to finish his call before a Tatar arrow pierced his throat. To commemorate the event the tune played by the trumpeter stops abruptly as if the life of the watchful guardian of the city came suddenly to an end (for a detailed description of the church see the chapter entitled "Wit Stwosz and St. Mary's Church").

In the centre of the Main Market Place stands the monumental long building of the **Cloth Hall** (16), with its enchanting arcades, Gothic brick walls and a Renaissance

Preserved old walls with the Florian Gate, today used by amateur artists and students of the nearby Academy of Fine Arts to display their work

Church and former monastery of St. Mark (corner of Sławkowska and św. Marka Streets), at present a home for retired priests. This building, begun in 1263, has preserved its original beauty despite four fires

Main Market Place. View of the tower of St. Mary's Church from which a trumpet bugle call is sounded every hour to the four quarters of the globe

parapet. Its oldest, underground part dates back to the Romanesque period. Under King Casimir the Great (1333—70), the old market hall was expanded. The beautiful Gothic gables also date from the 14th century. Following a great fire in 1555, the Cloth Hall was rebuilt in Renaissance style. Gianmaria Padovano topped it with a Polish parapet adorned with sculpted mascarons presumably by Santi Gucci of Florence. In the 19th century this imposing edifice was tidied up and renovated by the architect Tomasz Pryliński and with the completion of conservation work, Poland's first National Museum was opened on the first floor in 1879.

For centuries the wall high up under the arcades in the centre has borne a sword which once meant that the town was administered according to Magdeburg law and at the same time was a warning to evil-doers who were to be punished with it (hence its name, the "bloody sword"). This sword is associated with a legend about the two brothers who built the towers of St. Mary's. The elder brother noticed that the younger had built stronger foundations and his tower was rising higher and faster, and for this reason he murdered him with this sword. However he suffered from such acute pangs of conscience that eventually he committed suicide by jumping down from the tower.

In front of the Cloth Hall you can see the famous Cracow flower sellers, a stylish café and the **statue of Adam Mickiewicz** (17) designed in 1898 by Teodor Rygier, destroyed by the Nazis in 1940 and restored in 1955. At the foot of the monument poets read their verses during the annual Cracow Art Festival in June, while Christmas crèches are displayed during the traditional Christmas crib contest in early December.

The opposite side of the Market Place is overlooked by the **Town Hall Tower** (18), all that remains of an early 16th century town hall which was pulled down in the early 19th century. High on top of the tower you can see a gilded eagle that used to guard the headquarters of the old municipal authorities, and below it, the tower clocks. The tower houses a branch of the Historical Museum of the City of Cracow, with a display devoted to the history of the municipal authorities, and its cellars have been turned to the Maszkaron theatre of satire.

Close by, near Grodzka Street, the small **Church of St. Adalbert** (19), one of the oldest churches in Cracow, is hidden in a clump of trees. In 1957—67 it was thoroughly examined and the results confirmed the legend that it dates back to the 10th century (it is also said that here St. Adalbert gave his sermons before his missionary expedition to Prussia). The vaults contain a small display devoted to the history of the Market Place where you can trace the oldest pre-Romanesque stages of the construction of the church.

Many of the houses surrounding the Market Place are associated with important events in Polish history and culture. No. 6, called the **Grey House** (20), once the property of a magnate family, was visited by kings and served as the headquarters of the National Government during the Cracow uprising of 1846 and of Thaddeus Kosciuszko during the insurrection of 1794. Later for almost a hundred years it housed a tea and coffee shop run by the Szarski family, the best shop in this part of the country. The tablet on the façade of **no. 7** says that in 1558 it was the first Polish post office. **No. 8, Pod Jaszczurami** (Under the Salamanders) houses the popular "Jaszczury" student club. **No. 9** (21) once belonged to the richest banker family in the Renaissance period, the Boners. Here in 1605, a magnate's daughter, Maryna Mniszech, married the False Dimitri. Its most attractive feature is a richly carved parapet in Netherlandish style. **No. 13** (22), Pod Złotą Głową (Under the Gold Head), has had a pharmacy since 1403, and it is still there.

The southern side of the Market Place begins with **no. 14** (23), Pod św. Anną (Under St. Anne), the headquarters of the Cracow branch of the Polonia Society for Relations with Poles Resident Abroad. The neighbouring house belonged in the 14th century to the famous Cracow patrician family of Wierzynek. According to old records in 1364, during a royal congress in Cracow, one of the representatives of this family gave a magnificent feast in honour of Casimir the Great's guests. Today "Wierzynek" in the same house is Poland's best restaurant. No. 17 is the famous **Hetmans' House** (24) dating from the 14th century, where field hetmans used to live (crown hetmans had their residence on Wawel Hill). Earlier it had been a mint, today it houses the Museum of the History of Photography. The ground floor includes two attractive halls with Gothic cross and rib vaulting. In 1979 a 14th century Gothic door with a portal, the only well preserved items of their kind in Cracow, were discovered here. The house carries a plaque with a description of a great fire that ravaged Cracow in 1850. The corner house at Bracka Street changed hands repeatedly and hence is referred to by different names, the most common of them being the **Jabłonowski Mansion** (25).

At the corner of św. Anny street you can see the famous **Mansion Pod Baranami** (Under the Rams) (26) which is composed of several old Gothic houses that were joined together and converted in Renaissance style by Just Decius, secretary to King Sigismund (I) the Old. In the 19th and 20th centuries it belonged to the Potocki family. At present it houses the Cracow Community Centre together with, in the cellars, the renowned cabaret "Piwnica Pod Baranami". From the window of the **Spis Mansion** (27) at no. 34, King John III (Sobieski), having received the homage of the burghers, admired a display of fireworks and a popular festival. In the same building the first permanent public theatre was opened in 1781. The **Krzysztofory Mansion** (28) at no. 35, dating from 1635—40, like the Under the Rams Mansion, came into being as a result of conversion of three Gothic houses into a residence for the crown marshal Adam Kazanowski. Today, it is the headquarters of the Historical Museum of the City of Cracow, while its cellars contain an exhibition hall of the Cracow Group of artists.

The **house Pod Jeleniem** (Under the Stag) at no. 36 (29) at the corner of Sławkowska Street was once an excellent inn where, as the appropriate commemorative plaque says, Johann Wolfgang Goethe stopped during his stay in Cracow, as did Tsar Nicholas I. At no. 47 (30) **Pod Orłem** (Under the Eagle), Thaddeus Kosciuszko lived in 1777 when he was still a captain.

The Royal Tract continues along GRODZKA Street, which connects the Market Place with Wawel Hill, and which, next to Floriańska, is Cracow's oldest and most famous street. Though it is relatively short as many as eight churches are situated by it or in its close vicinity. Grodzka used to form a part of the trade route linking Cracow with Wieliczka, Bochnia and, farther afield, Hungary. Later on it joined Cracow with its neighbouring towns and villages: Kazimierz, Stradom and Okół. Following the great fire of 1850, which ravaged part of the Old Town, the stretch of Grodzka between the Market Place and the Dominican Square was broadened (before not even two carts could be accommodated side by side). In the 16th—17th centuries the house at no. 3 was occupied by Scharffenberg's printing press, while no. 4 was Siebeneycher's printing house where in 1597 the poet, translator and author Marcin Bielski published his *Polish Chronicle*. Both Scharffenberg and Siebeneycher were publishers and book sellers.

The vast square which Grodzka traverses has two names: its left hand side is called DOMINIKAŃSKI SQUARE after the Dominican church there, while the right hand side is WIOSNY LUDÓW SQUARE. The latter is adorned with two monuments standing in front of the **Wielopolski Mansion** (31), today the Office of the City of Cracow. They represent two famous city mayors, Mikołaj Zyblikiewicz, the mayor in 1874—81 (the work of W. Gadomski) and Józef Dietl, who held this office in 1866—74. The latter, designed by Xawery Dunikowski, is considered to be the best figural monument in Poland.

The **Franciscan church and monastery** (32), dating from the mid-13th century, are among the first brick structures in Cracow. The vaults of the church are the final resting place of Prince Boleslaus the Bashful (1243—79), and his sister,

Adam Mickiewicz statue in the Main Market Place, designed by Teodor Rygier, erected in 1898, destroyed by the Germans in 1940, restored in 1955. In the background, façade of St. Mary's Church

Display of the most attractive Christmas crèches held each December
by the Adam Mickiewicz statue. This annual competition enjoys
tremendous popularity among amateur artists, workers and young
people who build their Nativity scenes of cardboard, wood
and tin foil

Town Hall Tower, the only remaining fragment of the town hall
pulled down in the early 19th century. The tower, dating back to the
early 14th century, is 70 metres high and 50 cm out of perpendicular.
A branch of the Historical Museum of the City of Cracow, housing
a display on the history of the municipal authorities

Main Market Place where numerous meetings, manifestations and parades are held. In the photo: pageant of highlanders in regional costume

Annual enthronement of the new king of the Marksmen's Fraternity established over 700 years ago, held in the Main Market Place. In the photo: the new king is holding a silver cock, the emblem of the fraternity, a gift of the municipal authorities, dating from 1565. The cock, partly gilded and enamelled, is 42 cm in height

Lajkonik, a folk pageant about a brave raftsman who, having defeated the Tatar khan, put on the latter's robes and entered the city. In the Main Market Place he performs a dance with banners and drinks a cup of wine to the prosperity of the town and its inhabitants. This old custom is revived each year eight days before Corpus Christi

the Blessed Salomea. In the monastery, you can admire beautiful cloisters with, embedded in them, remains of gravestones, valuable Gothic polychromed paintings and a gallery of bishops' portraits beginning from the 15th century. There are several chapels of Cracow craftsmen's guilds dating from the same period. The church features eight stained-glass windows designed by Stanisław Wyspiański, representing the Blessed Salomea and St. Francis. Wyspiański's stained-glass above the choir loft, which shows God the Father the Creator, is regarded by experts as the most beautiful Polish stained-glass window. The same artist painted most of the polychromes in the chancel and the transept while the Stations of the Lord's Passions in the northern chapel are the work of Józef Mehoffer.

In front of the Franciscan church stands a statue of Cardinal Adam Sapieha, and on the opposite side, at 3 Franciszkańska Street, you can see the baroque **Bishops' Palace** (33) bearing on its façade a tablet commemorating the Polish pilgrimage of Pope John Paul II in 1979.

The Dominican Square is Cracow's oldest market place dating back to the period before 1257. The **Dominican church and monastery** (34) originated in the 13th century. The church has always had many wealthy benefactors including the most illustrious Polish families, the Lubomirskis, Przeździeckis, Sobieskis, Ligęzas, and Zbaraskis who built here their own chapels. The name of Santi Gucci is associated with the chapel endowed by the Myszkowski family. In 1289 the Cracow prince Leszek the Black was buried here. Here, too, a separate chapel contains the remains of St. Hiacinthus. The 14th century portal of the main entrance was later surrounded by a vestibule. The chancel boasts a bronze epitaph of Filip Kallimach (Philippo Buonaccorsi), dating from 1496 with a figure of the poet designed by Wit Stwosz. The beautiful 14th century stained-glass windows that used to adorn it have been deposited for safekeeping in the National Museum and can today be admired in the Szołayski Gallery at no. 9 Szczepański Square. The monastery has three garths, with the cloisters of the first of them dating from the 14th century, decorated with details of various monuments, gravestones and epitaphs. The monastery's rich archive (fortunately rescued from the fire which in 1850 ravaged the church, the tower and part of the monastery buildings) contains records beginning from the second half of the 13th century. The library, which once was just as rich, partly burnt down. The monastery treasury boasts a collection of Baroque religious painting, portraits of bishops, monstrances, ciboria, reliquaries and chasubles.

Farther along Grodzka Street, we must draw your attention to the emblem of the **Podelwie house** at no. 32 (35). This Gothic sculpture of a lion, dating from the 14th century, is recognized as the oldest emblem in Cracow. **No. 39** at the corner of Poselska Street (36) used to be the home of Wit Stwosz, as indicated by a special tablet on the building's façade.

Poselska, which crosses Grodzka, once formed the boundary of old Cracow (in 1257) for beyond it, in the direction of Wawel Hill, stretched the settlement of Okół incorporated into the town in the mid-14th century, when the town walls were shifted to the vicinity of Wawel.

If you turn left into Poselska Street, you will reach the charming site of the **Bernardine convent and St. Joseph's Church** (37), their origins going back to the 17th century; and the converted manor house of the Lanckoroński family. Later the convent was expanded to take in the manor houses of the Pieniążek and finally the Morsztyn families. In 1788 another Bernardine convent, from Stradom, was transferred to Poselska Street. The church has a Baroque-style décor.

The house at no. 53 Grodzka Street is the **Collegium Iuridicum** (38) where law professors of the Jagiellonian University used to live and teach. The Collegium dates back to the early 15th century and despite several conversions has preserved many magnificent Gothic features.

On the opposite side of the street, at **no. 52,** a Jesuit college was situated in the 17th century. Established during the Counter-Reformation period, it was meant to be a rival of the Jagiellonian University. Today, ironically enough, it is one of the university buildings. The **Church of St. Peter and St. Paul** next to it (39) is also associated with the Jesuits. Its construction was encouraged in 1597 by the famous Jesuit preacher Piotr Skarga Pawęski, who is buried in the crypt under the chancel. The wall around the church bears figures of the twelve apostles.

The nearby **Church of St. Andrew** (40) is one of the few Romanesque structures that have been preserved in good condition. Erected in the years 1079—98, it was a fortified building where, during the period of Tatar raids, the inhabitants of Okół sought refuge. The wall surrounding it is as old as the church. The interior is in Baroque style dating from the late 17th and early 18th centuries. The treasury contains many works of art, including figures and other elements of Nativity cribs dating back to the 14th century; these are among the oldest preserved figures in Europe.

At the end of Grodzka Street, at the foot of Wawel Hill, you can see the Romanesque **Church of St. Giles** (41), endowed presumably by Prince Ladislaus Herman (1076—1102) and his wife Judith of Bohemia, in thanksgiving for the birth of their son, Boleslaus, later King Boleslaus (III) Wrymouth. The present structure dates from the early 14th century. The last house on the left side of the street is the famous **Royal Arsenal** (42) built in the early 16th century by King Sigismund the Old. Of its original design an attractive portal has been preserved which today leads to the Geography Institute of the Jagiellonian University housed in the building.

THE OLD TOWN

The Small Market Place

The Small Market Place (Mały Rynek) was laid out as Cracow's second market place. It was situated in a slaughterers' quarter and used to serve as a meat market. Before the First World War it was turned into a fruit market. The houses on its eastern side have the kind of ground-floor terrace which once was also to be seen in front of the houses in the Main Market Place. Today such terraces are to be found only in the Small Market Place in Cracow and along Długa Street in Gdańsk.

The junction of Szpitalna and Mikołajska Streets with a view of the Small Market Place is a particularly attractive area. The imposing **house at no. 2** is in fact a mansion made from joining four Gothic houses together. These once contained an inn, an eating-house for beggars and two breweries. When they fell into ruin in the 18th century, they were all purchased by the wealthy merchant Lamelli who converted them into a mansion. During its renovation in 1975—79, magnificent Gothic polychrome paintings on religious subjects were discovered, the only such paintings to be seen in Cracow in a burgher's house. Today the Lamelli Mansion (43) houses the **City Centre Community Club.**

The **Szober House** (44) at no. 6 was once a printing press where in January 1661 the first Polish periodical, *Merkuriusz Polski,* appeared, **No. 4** houses the International Book and Press Club. Behind **houses nos. 3 to 5** stands the Gothic **Residential Tower** (45), a real architectural rarity, which at present is used by the Monument Conservation Department of the Academy of Fine Arts.

The western side of the Small Market Place is occupied by the Jesuit monastery and the Vicar's House, beyond the roofs of which you can see the towers and the chancel of St. Mary's Church and, through a passage, a prospect of St. Mary's (Mariacki) Square and St. Barbara's Church.

The Reformati Lane

In the past the **church and the monastery of the Reformati** (46) abutted the town walls. Today they stand by the Planty park. The entire complex of buildings is encircled by a high wall over which you can get a glimpse of the church roofs and towers. The main entrance is from Reformacka Street.

By the entrance to the Reformati church there is a bell for the dying — the only such bell so well preserved in Cracow — which, according to old custom, was tolled during the agony or shortly after the death of one of the monastery's inhabitants.

The Reformati arrived in Cracow in 1625 and initially settled in the suburb of Garbary. When in 1655 the Swedes besieged Cracow, the monks took shelter in the city and later moved there permanently. The church was built in 1622—73. Under the church there are vaults where, thanks to the extraordinary properties of the atmosphere, the bodies of the monks buried have become perfectly mummified. Apart from the monks, representatives of many celebrated Cracow families — the Wielopolskis, Morsztyns, Szembeks and Badenis — were also laid to rest here.

On the opposite side of Reformacka Street, in the shadow of old trees, you can see the Stations of the Cross painted in 1816 by Michał Stachowicz.

In a small square at the junction of Pijarska, św. Marka and Reformacka Streets the house at no. 8 bears a commemorative plaque saying that here, on 11 August 1944, the Gestapo arrested General Stanisław Rostworowski, the commander of the southern area of the underground Home Army.

Szczepański Square

Once this area was occupied by two churches, St. Szczepan's and the Church of St. Matthew and St. Maciej, and later by an army barracks. It has been a square, first a market place and at present a parking lot, for the past 200 years and is surrounded by a number of attractive though not particularly old buildings.

The square is separated from the Planty park by the **Palace of Art** (47), the headquarters of the Society of the Friends of the Fine Arts. It should be added that Cracow has over 450 various associations, this figure telling volumes about the atmosphere of the city and the diversity of interests of its inhabitants. The Society of the Friends of the Fine Arts came into being in 1854. Besides its headquarters at Szczepański Square, it has an attractive house at no. 6 Kanonicza Street, an art gallery in Nowa Huta and Jan Matejko's manor house at Krzesławice in Nowa Huta. The Palace of Art was built in 1901 and the mosaic frieze running along the entire length and breadth of the building is the work of Jacek Malczewski.

Opposite the Palace of Arts stands a pavilion with a sharply textured concrete façade. This building, popularly called the Bunker, is the venue of the International Graphic Art Biennale. The corner of Jagiellońska Street is occupied by the **Stary (Old) Theatre** named after Helena Modrzejewska (Modjeska) (48); the company has earned international reputation and appeared all over the world. It is Poland's oldest theatre building still in use. It came into being as a result of joining together two houses and was opened on 1 January 1799. Following reconstruction carried out between 1830 and 1843, it resumed operation on 1 January 1843. After a new municipal theatre (now the Juliusz Słowacki Theatre) was completed in 1893 at Szpitalna Street, the building at Jagiellońska was again thoroughly renovated and modernized and its façade was given a fashionable Art Nouveau appearance.

The true gem of Szczepański Square is the **Szołayski House** at no. 9 (49), donated by the Szołayski family to the National Museum in the early 20th century. Today, the house is a branch of the museum with a collection of Polish guild art dating from between the 15th and 18th centuries. The façade of the Szołayski House carries a tablet with the former name of the square, the National Guard Square.

Św. Ducha Square

In the past this square was occupied by hospitals (hence the name of the nearby street, Szpitalna) as well as the monastery and church of the Holy Spirit. The first Cracow

Work is going on on the restoration and conservation of Cracow's historic buildings. In the photo: restored houses with the Wierzynek restaurant in the Main Market Place

hospital was established in 1244. Unfortunately in 1891, when plans were drawn up to build a new municipal theatre, the majority of old hospital buildings were demolished, despite protests from the public. Thanks to the efforts of conservators, the remaining buildings were skilfully restored and today this square is really charming and picturesque. Its most magnificent feature is the **Church of the Holy Cross** (50) dating from circa 1300. Inside, you may admire marvellous palm vaulting resting on a single column and beautiful Renaissance polychrome paintings.

The part of the square that borders on św. Marka Street is occupied by an old Gothic house Pod Krzyżem (Under the Cross), today a branch of the Historical Museum of the City of Cracow with a display devoted to the history of the Cracow theatre.

Cracow's best restaurant, Wierzynek, is housed in attractive historic interiors. Wierzynek was a Cracow patrician who in 1364 gave a splendid feast for King Casimir the Great's guests

Courtyard of the Bishops' Palace with the statue of John Paul II
designed by Ione Sensi Croci, 1980

Palace of Cracow Bishops in Franciszkańska Street, beginning on
30 December 1963 the residence of the 76th bishop of Cracow, Karol
Wojtyła, who in 1978 left it to attend the conclave in Rome where he
was elected Pope and took the name of John Paul II. In 1944, lectures
of the secret theological department of the Jagiellonian University
were held here

The treasury of St. Andrew's Church (Grodzka Street) — one of the oldest Romanesque churches, magnificently preserved — contains sixteen figures and other elements of 14th century Nativity scenes

14th century Nativity crib, a gift of Elizabeth, the wife of King Ladislaus the Short, sister of Casimir the Great, for St. Andrew's Church

Church of St. Peter and St. Paul in Grodzka Street. Its origins are associated with the Jesuits who were brought to Poland to combat the Reformation. Modelled on Rome's del Gesù, it was built between 1597 and 1635

Small Market Place with a view of the chancel of St. Mary's and the Church of St. Barbara

Mariacki (St. Mary's) Square

This square was laid out in 1802 in place of the old parish cemetery that used to surround St. Mary's Church. The square has a small pigeon font, and the houses around it, especially along its northern side, respresent typically bourgeois architecture. **No. 3,** called Hippolitów (Hippolits') (51), features such well preserved interiors that after restoration it will be turned into a branch of the Historical Museum devoted to the "bourgeois interior". The corner house at Szpitalna Street is the Prelate's House, built in 1618—19, where you can admire a wealth of period furniture and paintings by excellent artists. The building is topped by what is regarded as a typically Cracow parapet.

Farther in the square stands the **Church of St. Barbara** (52), endowed in 1338 by Mikołaj Wierzynek, a representative of a rich Cracow patrician family. This church, originally a cemetery chapel, has been repeatedly converted; Gothic, however, still predominates in its architecture. Next to the entrance, you can see Gethsemane, a group of stone sculptures showing Christ with three apostles, the work of artists from the circle of Wit Stwosz.

The façade of the **house at no. 8,** at the height of the first storey, bears a bas-relief representation of Christ in Gethsemane, a copy of Wit Stwosz's original which its owner, the merchant Ludwik Halski, offered to the National Museum. The neighbouring house, **no. 9,** carries a commemorative plaque saying that in the house that stood on this site Stanisław Wyspiański in 1907 wrote his best known drama, *The Wedding.*

Gródek

Today merely a hillock, it was once a fairly high promontory with, on top of it, the fortified manor house of Albert, Cracow administrator and Wieliczka salt master, who in 1311, during the invasion of the Bohemian King John of Luxemburg, betrayed Prince Ladislaus the Short.

The Polish prince defeated the invading army, liberated Cracow and dealt severely with the rebels. In place of Albert's manor house he had built a small castle the garrison of which was charged with keeping watch over the burghers' loyalty. Having changed hands several times, the castle was converted into a Dominican monastery. Next to it, the **Church of Our Lady of the Snows** (53) was built; here you can admire an attractive 17th century pulpit. The monastery wall facing the Planty park has a picture of Our Lady of the Snows who, as legend has it, in 1655 shielded Cracow from the Swedes with her own cloak.

Kanonicza Street

This is generally regarded as the most attractive street in old Cracow. Though its name derives from the canons of the Cracow cathedral who once lived here, in the past it also had many knightly manors. In the course of research carried before the complete restoration of the entire street it was discovered that all houses had Renaissance loggias, cloisters, portals and polychrome paintings, frequently hidden under layers of later accretions. Many of the houses feature beautiful portals with armorial cartouches emblazoned with a sculpted cardinal's hat and three crowns: the emblem of Wawel cathedral.

The **house at no. 1** dates back to the 14th century, although in the 16th century it was thoroughly reconstructed as the residence of Bishop Ignacy Maciejowski. During the period of the Republic of Cracow, it was the Inquisitorial Court of the Free City of Cracow and a prison. After the restoration of this now seriously damaged building is completed, it will be turned over to one of Cracow's cultural institutions.

The **house at no. 2** is topped by a crenellated parapet, one of the rare examples of this type in Cracow. **No. 3** is a former hospice for students from the nearby Collegium Iuridicum. **No. 5** was built by Jan Długosz, a 15th century chronicler and tutor to the royal children. **No. 6** used to be a knightly residence and today belongs to the Society of the Friends of the Fine Arts (54). **No. 7** is the headquarters of the Cracow branch of the Polish Writers' Union. The occupants of the **house at no. 9** included Father Hugo Kołłątaj (1750—1812), a statesman, author and thinker of the Enlightenment period and rector of the Jagiellonian University, as well as Władysław Ludwik Anczyc (1829—83), an author of patriotic plays. At present the building is a branch of the National Museum with a display devoted to Stanisław Wyspiański. **No. 18** features a sumptuous Renaissance portal ascribed to Jan Michałowicz of Urzędów, called the Polish Praxiteles.

The **Chapter House** (55) at no. 19 dates from the 15th century, however owing to numerous conversions its present façade carries classicist features. During investigation carried out in 1977 it was discovered that the house used to have a beautiful Renaissance courtyard. It was in this house, and later in the Dean's House next door, at no. 21, that the priest, then titular bishop of Ombia and suffragan of Cracow, Karol Wojtyła, the present Pope John Paul II, lived. The Dean's House is a finely preserved Renaissance residence of the deans of the chapter. Built in 1582—88 by Santi Gucci, it has an arcaded courtyard with a sculpted representation of Bishop St. Stanislaus in the centre.

The **house at no. 25** at the corner of Podzamcze Street, is the former royal bath-house of Ladislaus Jagiello and beginning in 1450, the residence of Jan Długosz, who wrote here his magnum opus, the *Annales seu cronicae incliti regni Poloniae*. The façade of the house features a 17th century picture of the Madonna with traces of bullets going back, according to tradition, to the times of the Swedish invasion, a commemorative tablet from 1480, and another tablet, saying that in the 19th century the house contained the studio of the sculptor Franciszek Wyspiański, the father of the poet and painter Stanisław, who spent his childhood here, at the foot of Wawel Hill.

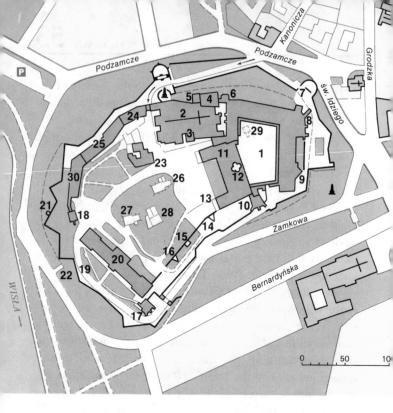

1. Arcaded courtyard; 2. Cathedral; 3. Sigismund Chapel; 4. Cathedral
Treasury; 5. Sigismund Tower; 6. Sobieski Tower; 7. Tower
of Sigismund III Vasa; 8. Hen's Foot Tower; 9. Danish Tower;
10. Senator's Tower; 11. Former royal kitchens; 12. Rotunda
of St. Felix and St. Adauctus; 13. Entrance to the exhibition "Wawel
That Is no More"; 14. Tęczyński's Tower; 15. Nobleman's Tower;
16. Maiden's Tower; 17. Sandomierz Tower; 18. Thief's Tower;
19. Foundations of mediaeval walls; 20. Former Austrian barracks;
21. Descent to the Dragon's Cave; 22. Entrance to the Dragon's Cave;
23. Vicar's House; 24. Cathedral Museum; 25. Former theological
seminary; 26. Foundations of St. Michael's Church; 27. Foundations
of St. George's Church; 28. Foundations of Borek's house;
29. Foundations of a pre-Romanesque structure; 30. Conservation
workshops

WAWEL HILL

You can get the finest view of Wawel Hill, its castle, cathedral, towers and walls, and the menacing cannon aimed at the town, from a square at the end of Grodzka and Waryńskiego Streets, while approaching the hill from Kanonicza Street, you will see a bronze equestrian statue of Thaddeus Kosciuszko standing on a bastion called the Ladislaus IV bastion.

Once Wawel was the residence of Polish princes and later kings. The hill has been witness to the thousand year old history of the Polish nation and Wawel has become a symbol of the Poland of the Piasts under whose rule the country developed and of the Jagiellons, when it experienced a period of greatness. Annually it is visited by millions of tourists who come here to learn the history of their own nation.

Wawel Hill forms an immensely large complex of buildings and exhibition halls. What then should you see first and foremost in order to get the best possible knowledge of this most famous historic monument in Poland? First, the royal castle and cathedral, as well as the Cathedral Museum and all the other exhibitions in the castle, and the legendary Dragon's Cave.

THE ROYAL CASTLE

Wawel Hill covers an area of some 15 acres. Between the 8th and 10th centuries it was a stronghold town of the Wiślanie tribe and perhaps the residence of that "mightily powerful prince" who is mentioned in *The Life of St. Methodius* dating from the 9th century. Towards the end of the 10th century it definitely became one of the royal residences and in the year 1000, the seat of the bishops of Cracow. We know that it had a mint, a state treasury, a garrison of retainers, a prison, a cathedral school, a mound where court trials were held, and residential houses. Its protection against enemies were powerful earthworks reinforced with timber and stone.

The architectural history of Wawel Hill can be roughly divided into three periods each of which left behind its own specific mark: (1) the reign of Boleslaus the Brave (992—1025); (2) of Casimir the Great (1333—70); and (3) of Sigismund the Old (1506—48) and Sigismund Augustus (1548—72), also referred to as the Sigismund period.

In circa 1020 Boleslaus the Brave began the construction of the first stone cathedral. This was followed by a palatium together with a rotunda chapel dedicated to the Blessed Virgin Mary (later to St. Felix and St. Adauctus) and a quadrangular, either residential or sepulchral, structure. During the 11th and 12th centuries other buildings were erected. Finally a Romanesque stone residential and defensive complex with a keep was built. In 1320 the construction of the third cathedral, Gothic in style, began.

Until the reign of Casimir the Great Wawel was a fortified residence of the senior princes and kings of Poland. Under Casimir the Great it experienced one of its periods of development and expansion, which was connected with the reorganization of the state and with the consolidation of Cracow's role as the capital. Casimir the Great, famous for the protection he extended to art and science and for his ventures in the field of architecture, turned the old Romanesque structure into a powerful Gothic castle.

Following a fire in 1500, King Sigismund the Old had the castle converted into a Renaissance residence worthy of the powerful Jagiellonian state. Wawel became the centre of state, scientific and cultural life, the site of major Seym sessions and other important political events. The royal residence was ornamented by the best European artists, masons, and sculptors from Italy, Germany and Poland.

Later, following two dangerous fires in 1595, the castle was reconstructed in early Baroque style. Unfortunately, with the transfer of the royal residence to Warsaw, it was visited by the royal family less and less frequently and systematically stripped of its furnishings.

The Swedish invasions of 1655—57 devastated the castle. The Swedes, and then the Prussians, Austrians and Russians in the 18th century, plundered what had remained of the former splendour of the royal residence.

During the partitions of Poland, when Cracow found itself under the rule of Austria, the castle and some other buildings on Wawel Hill were turned into a barracks and a military hospital, while some structures, including two Gothic churches, were pulled down in order to provide room for parade grounds. The castle became a barracks and the Austrians planned to convert the castle chambers into "small cells for soldiers" and to transfer the royal sarcophagi and coffins from the cathedral to the Church of St. Peter and St. Paul.

Following years of efforts, the Poles managed to purchase Wawel from Austrian hands and the Austrian army finally left Wawel Hill in 1911. Immediately work began on restoring the whole complex (conservation work in the castle had been completed earlier). A new wave of disasters came with the Nazi occupation. The castle became the residence of the Governor General Hans Frank. The royal stables and kitchens were pulled down and the Gothic chambers of Casimir the Great were turned into an ale-house, the Senators' Hall into a cinema and the garden terraces into a swimming pool. Many works of art were lost or taken to Germany.

Immediately after the liberation in 1945, conservation work was resumed with the help of state funds, and the restoration of the castle was completed. The historic items amassed at Wawel form the most valuable collection in all Poland.

The castle has 71 rooms with a total surface area of over

7,000 sq. metres. Its interiors, which form a museum called the Wawel State Art Collections, contain five major exhibitions:

1. The royal rooms and chambers appointed in the style of the Jagiellon and Vasa eras;
2. The Royal Treasury;
3. The Castle Armoury;
4. The East in the Wawel Collections; and
5. Wawel That Is no More.

The inscription above the main gate says: *Si Deus nobiscum, quis contra nos* (When God is with us, who is against us). A long gateway passage leads into an **arcaded Renaissance courtyard** (1) which provided a model for many architects in their designs of various magnate residences. The loggias in the courtyard are the work of Francesco Fiorentino and date from 1507—36. In the past the courtyard was the site of jousting contests and court events; today various spectacles, concerts and theatre performances are held here. Under the roof along the loggias, there is a frieze painted in 1536 by Dionizy Stuba.

The ground floor of the castle used to serve as the

Eastern view of the Royal Castle on Wawel Hill

Noua Turris.
Palacia S.R.M.tis
S. Staniflai
Stabula
S.R.M.tis
Lataranea

North-western view of Wawel Hill according to a copperplate in
J. Braun and A. Hoghenberg's *Civitates orbis terrarum. Liber sextus,*
Cologne 1618

servants' quarters, the chancery, the court rooms and the
treasury. The royal chambers were to be found on the first
and second floor. The most valuable items to be-seen in the
castle are the Arrases. The first series of them, composed of
sixteen pieces, was commissioned in Antwerp in 1523 by

Castle. Northern and eastern wings seen from the arcaded courtyard (1507—36)

Castle. Early Baroque royal chapel of the Vasas on the second floor (1602—03) with 16th and 17th century stucco decoration and Italian furniture

Castle. The Deputies' Chamber. The coffered ceiling with male and female heads, originally 194 in all, sculpted by Sebastian Tauerbach and Jan Janda, polychromed by Andrzej Jungholcz (1531—35). In the photo: a female head in a coif and with a band across her mouth

King Sigismund the Old, but the majority were purchased by Sigismund Augustus on whose death the collection numbered 356 pieces. The size of the individual Arrases corresponds to the size of the castle chambers and their subject matter must have been carefully selected. During the period of the partitions their fate was lamentable: they were looted and scattered in various countries, only part of the original collection returning to Poland in 1922—26. They survived the Second World War in Canada and were restored to their former place only in 1961. The present collection comprises 143 pieces.

Many pieces of furniture go back to Gothic times. There are Italian, French, German and English pieces, including beautiful clocks, the oldest of which, a table clock with a dome, dates from 1589. The portrait gallery includes likenesses of Sigismund the Old, the founder of the Renaissance castle, his son Sigismund Autustus to whom Wawel owes its collection of tapestries, his daughter Anne

Castle. Detail of the tapestry *The Story of Eden* from the series "The Story of Adam and Eve", before 1553, 463 by 854 cm

Castle. Tapestry, for hanging above the window, with the Polish coat-of-arms and animals, after 1553, 68 by 254 cm

Castle. *Pietà*, by an unknown 16th century painter of the south Netherlandish school. Oil on wood, 43.5 by 31 cm

Castle. *The Madonna with Child*, by Sebastiano Mainardi (?), late 15th century. Tempera on wood, 52 by 42 cm

the Jagiellon and his son-in-law, King Stephen Báthory, and a portrait of the future King Sigismund III Vasa as a child. There are also valuable paintings on historical and religious subjects.

The Royal Treasury

The Royal Treasury, which occupies the ground-floor Gothic rooms dating back to the period of Casimir the Great and Ladislaus Jagiello, houses a display of the crown jewels and national mementos as well as other valuable

Castle. *Caritas*, by an unknown mid-16th century painter of the south Netherlandish school. Oil on wood, 78 by 62 cm

STANISLAVS COMES IN TEN:
CZYN IOANNIS PALATINI
RAC. VLTIMI VIRORVM
DE TENCZYN FILIVS

Castle. Majolica vase. Patanazzi workshop, Urbino, late 16th century

◄ Castle. *Portrait of Stanisław Tęczyński*, by Tommaso Dolabella (?), before 1634. Oil on canvas, 195 by 108 cm

Castle. Interior of a circular Turkish tent. Canvas, damask, canvas and leather appliqué work, 17th century

Castle. Royal Treasury. Chalice with paten from the abbey of Tyniec near Cracow, mid-11th century. Gold, height of the chalice 8.8 cm, diameter of the cup 6.6 cm, diameter of the paten 8.7 cm

Castle. Royal Treasury. "Szczerbiec" (Jagged Sword), coronation sword of the Polish kings, 13th century. Steel blade, hilt of gold sheet, 98.4 cm in length

Castle. Royal Treasury. Pendant of rock crystal set in gold, discovered in 1964 during archaeological excavations on Wawel Hill, 10th—11th century. Height 5.6 cm, width 1.5 cm, length of the chain 12.8 cm

Castle. Royal Treasury. Ceremonial hat with a representation of the Holy Spirit, a gift of Pope Innocent XI to King John III (Sobieski) following the victory at Vienna in 1683. Velvet embroidered in gold and pearls, height 26.5 cm

Castle. Royal Armoury. Hussar's half-armour with an original pair
of wings. Poland, 17th century

objects in gold, silver and ivory, and costly clocks. Unfortunately the oldest and most precious crown jewels are not there since in 1795, following the collapse of the Kosciuszko insurrection, they were stolen by the Prussians and destroyed. Only the Szczerbiec (the Jagged Sword), the coronation sword of the Polish kings dating from 1320, returned safely to Wawel, perhaps because it contains little gold and a lot of iron; it is now the pride of the Royal Treasury. Other valuable objects include a Renaissance sword that was once used to dub knights and the coronation cloak of Sigismund Augustus. The oldest items are a rock crystal pendant from the late 10th or early 11th century and a chalice and paten from the 11th century that belonged to the abbots of Tyniec.

The Royal Armoury

The treasury has always been connected with the castle armoury where saddles and trappings, buzdygan maces, zigschakes, sabres and armour were stored. The first plans to revive the old armoury were drawn up before the Second World War but it was only in 1963 that through purchases and donations some 500 items of arms and armour were collected. These are mostly Polish and eastern — the latter mainly Turkish — items associated with King John III's wars. An interesting feature of the Armoury is replicas of the banners of the Teutonic Knights captured in 1410 in the battle of Grunwald. Their appearance was immortalized on parchment by the royal painter and illuminator Stanisław Durink and described by the 15th century chronicler Jan Długosz in his *Banderia Prutenorum.* The Armoury is housed in specially adapted premises, including a hall with its vaulting resting on one pillar, which dates back to the times of Casimir the Great. The adjustment of these rooms to serve a new purpose was not an easy task but the effort proved worthwhile for in the process workers uncovered outer Romanesque walls of the keep and of the residential tower, the lower storey of which is the armoury hall with its vaulting resting on one pillar.

The East in the Wawel Collections

The oriental items are displayed in the western wing of the castle and include Poland's largest collection, which is also one of the largest in the world, of 17th—18th century Turkish and Persian tents which are shown the way they were once erected in the field. Visitors are allowed to enter them to admire the richness and colour of the ornaments since their outside walls are grey and not particularly attractive. Besides the tents, there are also Turkish banners of considerable historic value, captured at Vienna and Parkany, precious eastern carpets, Persian and Turkish arms and armour, saddles and trappings.

Wawel That Is no More

We also recommend a visit to the **architectural reserve** (13) which presents pre-historic traces of man's activity going back to 50,000 years B.C. Finally the area of the former royal kitchens has been turned into a display devoted to the history of Wawel Hill, featuring various details that have been discovered on this site as well as the foundations of the oldest structures.

*

The individual items at Wawel are displayed to the best advantage. They are placed in a way that makes it possible to take a closer look at each of them.

By 1939 the collection numbered 2,200 items in all. The present collection includes 7,000 items, some of them purchased with state funds and many private donations from people in Poland and abroad.

Thanks to careful and competent selection and display the Wawel collection presents a considerable historic value and artistic merit, owing to which Wawel — the royal castle and the cathedral — is regarded as one of the leading collections admired by arrivals from all over the world.

THE CATHEDRAL

"Within its venerable walls Wawel cathedral holds the entire Polish past, that most glorious and most splendid past that is truly commendable, worth of following and deserving of eternal remembrance," wrote Karol Cardinal Wojtyła, the present Pope John Paul II.

Wawel Cathedral (2), a witness to the thousand years of Polish history, was the site of royal coronations and burials of Polish kings and members of their families.

The Cracow bishopric was established in the year 1000 and in circa 1020 the construction of the first stone cathedral began. This cathedral is referred to as Boleslaus the Brave's cathedral since it was this king that presumably began its construction. The second cathedral, which was considerably larger and had a nave and two aisles and two square towers, was built to the west of the first one in the years 1090—1142. When this was burnt down by a fire in 1305, Bishop Nanker undertook the construction, in 1320, of a third, Gothic cathedral completed as late as 1364 under King Casimir the Great. The imposing main door to the cathedral, with the recurring letter "K" for Kazimierz (Casimir), is a gift of Casimir the Great endowed on the occasion of the consecration of the shrine.

Each old historic building lives and acquires new elements as the new epochs and new styles come and go. This is immediately apparent in the décor of the cathedral which, though basically austere and Gothic, displays Renaissance order and Baroque exuberance. Owing to the cramped space on Wawel Hill that prevented its enlargement, it has preserved its original Gothic form, but is surrounded by chapels that were added in later periods. Viewed from the outside, these chapels form one beautiful, picturesque whole and each of them deserves a visit due to the wealth of works of art by outstanding Polish, Italian, German and Ruthenian artists held within.

Our tour of the cathedral begins in the right aisle where we pass in succession the chapels of the Holy Cross, the

Potockis, the Szafraniec family, the Vasas, Sigismund, Jan Konarski, Jakub Zadzik, King John Albert and Bishop Andrzej Załuski. The high altar is surrounded by the chapels of Bishop Piotr Tomicki, St. Mary and Bishop Piotr Gamrat. By the left aisle going from the main entrance, you will see the chapels of Queen Sophia (of the Holy Trinity), the Czartoryskis, the former chapel of St. Nicholas, the chapels of Bishop Samuel Maciejowski, the Lipskis, the Skotnickis, Bishop Andrzej Zebrzydowski, and the Sacristy.

The most beautiful and the most famous of them all is the **Sigismund Chapel** (Kaplica Zygmuntowska) (3) built between 1519 and 1533 on the orders of King Sigismund the Old by the Italian architect Bartolommeo Berrecci, with its interior decorated by Giovanni Cini, Gianmaria Padovano, Niccolo da Castiglione, Antonio and Philippo de Fiesole, Bernardino di Zanobi de Gianotis and Giovanni Soli. The result is what is generally considered to be the most beautiful Renaissance chapel to be seen north of the Alps.

The nave is separated from the chancel by a chapel built in 1628—30 according to a design by Giovanni Trevano in place of an old Gothic altar. This chapel and mausoleum contains the shrine of St. Stanislaus of Szczepanów, the bishop of Cracow canonized in 1253. The ashes of the saint were transferred to a sumptuous reliquary endowed by the Blessed Kinga and deposited in the centre of the cathedral by Bishop Prandota and Prince Boleslaus the Bashful. The first coffin of Saint Stanislaus was in the form of a Romanesque chest, the second was endowed by Queen Jadwiga, and the third by King Sigismund III. The present coffin dates from 1669—71 and is the work of Peter van der Rennen of Gdańsk. Following the ancient Greek and Roman tradition the grave of Saint Stanislaus became the altar of the country — *Ara Patriae*, where kings deposited banners captured from the enemy, for example in the battles of Płowce in 1331, Grunwald in 1410 and Vienna in 1683. The present marble altar was endowed in 1783 by the suffragan Franciszek Potkański and the Cracow chapter.

The chancel has late Renaissance stalls and a pulpit, both the work of the carpenter Jan Szabur dating from 1620, and a Baroque altar also going back to the 17th century.

In 1320 the cathedral began to perform the role of a coronation church and in 1333 became a royal necropolis. The first king to have been buried here was Ladislaus the Short who died in 1333. A dozen or so years later his son, Casimir the Great, honoured his father with an imposing monument which served as a model for the other mediaeval sarcophagi in the cathedral.

In the southern ambulatory next to the high altar you can see the sarcophagus of King Casimir the Great (d. 1370), a fine red tomb under a canopy, with arcades, figures and inscriptions, which is thought to be the work of Hungarian stone-masons influenced by French art. The third Gothic sarcophagus is the tomb of Ladislaus Jagiello (d. 1434) to the right of the main entrance. It is covered with a Renaissance canopy resting on eight columns, the work of Giovanni Cini of Siena. Ladislaus Jagiello was the last monarch to be buried in the nave. His successors were laid to rest in the chapels. The sarcophagus of King Casimir the Jagiellon (d. 1492), one of the masterpieces of Wit Stwosz, is to be seen in the Holy Cross Chapel.

Between the times of Ladislaus the Short and 1795, that is the end of the Commonwealth, nearly all monarchs were buried in the crypts of Wawel Cathedral. Since the royal coffins, especially those of the Jagiellons and the Vasas, are genuine masterpieces sumptuously adorned with sculptures, in 1873 the vaults were put in order and opened to the public. During the partition period, when there were no more kings of Poland, in order to put heart into the people national heroes were buried here. For example in the Romanesque crypt of St. Leonard (1050—1118), Prince Joseph Poniatowski was buried in 1817 and Thaddeus Kosciuszko in 1818. Later spiritual leaders of the Polish nation were laid to rest in the cathedral crypts, Adam Mickiewicz in 1890 and Juliusz Słowacki in 1927. In 1935 Marshal Józef Piłsudski was buried in the cathedral crypt.

The Cathedral Treasury

The **Cathedral Treasury** (4), one of the most precious and richest church treasuries in Poland, occupies a Gothic building dating from 1481—1500, next to the cathedral (entrance through the Sacristy). Since the 11th century the treasury has collected liturgical vessels and vestments and national mementos. Unfortunately, two raids by the Swedish army (in 1657 and 1702) as well as contributions imposed by Russia and Austria considerably depleted its resources. Also many valuable objects were donated in support of the national cause during Kosciuszko's insurrection. According to an inventory, in 1563 the treasury contained 300 chalices, numerous crosses and monstrances, 150 candle-holders and over 600 sumptuously embroidered and decorated vestments. The showpieces of the collection are the spear of St. Maurice which in the year 1000 Boleslaus the Brave was offered by the Holy Roman Emperor Otto III, a magnificent gold reliquary for the head of St. Stanislaus (1504), a cross made from the crowns of Boleslaus the Bashful (d. 1279) and the Blessed Kinga (d. 1292), many fine chasubles, the oldest of which, dating from 1504, was a gift of the grand marshal of the crown, Piotr Kmita, and is presumed to be the work of Stanisław Stwosz, as well as mitres, regalia and historic mementos.

The Cathedral Museum

In 1978, in the Gothic building opposite the entrance to the cathedral, a new museum (24) was opened with a display of objects which had been kept in the cathedral treasury, the library and the chapter archives. The most valuable items are still deposited in the treasury and only replicas of them are put on display in the museum. The museum has a large collection of objects associated with the cult of Bishop St. Stanislaus, as well as replicas of royal funebral insignia (the originals remain in the graves). A separate room is devoted to documents and objects connected with Pope John Paul II who as cardinal metropolitan of Cracow supported the idea of establishing this museum.

The Chapter Archives and Library

The entrance to this part of the Wawel complex leads through the former chapel of St. Nicholas. According to an inventory carried out in 1110, the library, one of the oldest in Poland, had as many as 53 volumes. At present, it has 230 handwritten codices, while the annals and calendars amassed here date as far back as the 13th century. One of the showpieces is the so-called *Emmeram Gospel Book* from Regensburg, which dates from the early 12th century. In the course of centuries the collection has become enlarged through donations by kings, bishops, canons and aristocrats. Th manuscripts, incunabula (some 170 items) and old prints (about 500 items) from the library constitute an invaluable source of information for students of the history of Polish culture.

The Towers

The Wawel towers have always overlooked a panorama of Cracow. They were the highest of all and by tradition no other tower in the city could be taller than them. The cathedral has three towers: the Silver Bells' or Vicar's Tower, with its lower part built of Romanesque stone and the upper section of stone and brick dating from the 14th century; the bronze of the bells of this tower contains a high silver admixture, hence its name; the Clock (or Solomon's) Tower built in the third quarter of the 14th century and adorned with figures of St. St. Casimir, Wenceslas, Stanislaus and Adalbert; and the Sigismund Tower adjoining the treasury, which contains the famous Sigismund Bell.

The **Sigismund Tower** (5), entered through the Sacristy, was originally a defensive tower (second half of the 14th century) and became a church tower in 1412. Of the old bells it contains, the best known is the Sigismund Bell, cast in 1520 by Jan Beham and endowed by King Sigismund the Old whose name it bears. The Sigismund Bell is sounded on the most solemn church and state occasions when it can be heard all over Cracow.

The most notable of the castle towers are the **Senator's** (also known as Lubranka) (10), **Tęczyński's** (14), **Thief's** (18), **Maiden's** (16), **Nobleman's** (15) and **Danish** (9) **towers.** The underground part of the Senator's tower is a deep dungeon where once the most dangerous criminals were imprisoned. Its walls still carry various 17th century inscriptions such as "A thousand years and ten thousand is not" or "This is where my misdoings have brought me".

The Dragon's Cave

Legend has it that once upon a time a dragon belching fire lived in a huge cave under Wawel Hill. Every week he had to be given several head of cattle or else he would eat people. King Krak (Krakus) who reigned in Cracow promised his daughter and the throne to anyone who would kill the monster. A brave cobbler called Skuba came forward. He filled a lamb's hide with burning sulphur and left it right next to the cave. The dragon ate it and soon the castle and the city were shaken by a powerful roaring. The monster reached the river and started drinking water until it burst. Such was the end of the dragon while in the castle a sumptuous wedding party took place.

Every Polish child knows this legend. Indeed, there is a large cave under Wawel Hill, entered from the side of the Vistula. In front of the cave (22) stands a large bronze dragon. Visitors can enter the cave through a passageway (21) high up next to the Thief's Tower. In the 16th century the cave was occupied by an inn with a brothel. And although in 1565 King Sigismund Augustus ordered it to be bricked over, it was again in operation in the 17th and 18th centuries. It was very conveniently situated, next to the ford across the river. In the 19th century the cave stood empty,

Southern view of the cathedral

Cathedral. Golden dome of the Sigismund Chapel, built as a sepulchral chapel in 1517—33 according to a design by and under the supervision of Bartolommeo Berrecci. Seen from the south-east

but still constituted a considerable attraction so that during his stay in Cracow in 1880 the Emperor Francis Joseph expressed his desire to see it, and his wishes were, of course, complied with.

Today, after safety work had been completed, the Dragon's Cave is again open to the public. Beyond it there are five caves more, although the passages are so narrow that they can be entered only by potholers.

Cathedral. Statue of St. Stanislaus on the late Baroque dome of the Clock Tower

Cathedral. Detail of the figure of King Casimir the Jagiellon on the slab of the sarcophagus, sculpted in marble by Wit Stwosz (1492—94)

Cathedral. Interior of the Sigismund Chapel with the sarcophagi of Kings Sigismund the Old and Sigismund Augustus

Cathedral. The Adoration of the Magi, detail of the silver altar in the Sigismund Chapel, wrought silver sheet, made in 1531—38 by Melchior Baier who modelled his work in part on Albrecht Dürer's woodcuts

Cathedral. The crypt of the cathedral contains the mortal remains of most of the Polish kings as well as national heroes and bards

Cathedral. The Holy Cross Chapel. Polychromy dating from circa 1470, painted by Ruthenian artists from the circle of the Novgorod school (Pskov school); despite strenuous conservation work this is irretrievably fading away. In the photo: detail of the ceiling painting

Cathedral. Poland's most famous bell, Sigismund, endowed in 1520 by King Sigismund the Old, cast by Jan Beham. It is sounded only on particularly solemn church and state occasions

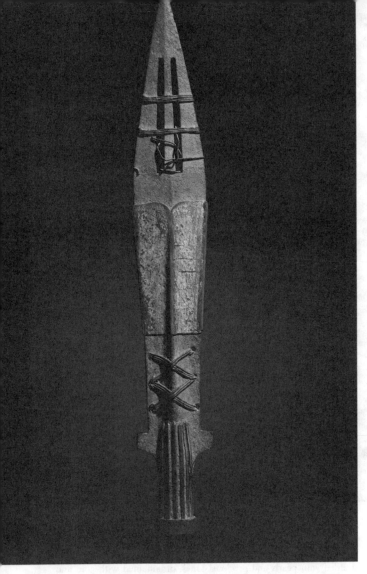

Cathedral. Cathedral Treasury. St. Maurice's spear offered in 1000 in Gniezno to King Boleslaus the Brave by the Holy Roman Emperor Otto III. Iron, fittings of gilded copper, length 50.5 cm, breadth 7 cm

Cathedral. The Holy Cross Chapel. *The Madonna and Child*, detail of the Ruthenian polychrome painting, circa 1470

Cathedral. The Holy Cross Chapel. Panel of the Holy Cross Triptych with a representation of the Chorus of Apostles, produced in 1467 in Cracow

Cathedral. Cathedral Museum. Cross made in 1472—88 of two crowns of presumed Venetian provenance dating from the 13th century, originally belonging to Prince Boleslaus the Bashful (d. 1279) and his wife the Blessed Princess Kinga (d. 1292). Wood lined with gold sheet, studded with pearls and precious stones, ornamented with gold and enamel, 83.8 by 58 cm

Cathedral. Cathedral Museum. Romanesque cross dating from the 13th century, a gift of Cardinal Mieczysław Ledóchowski in 1878. Silver

Cathedral. Cathedral Treasury. Reliquary for the skull of St. Stanislaus in the form of a tin decorated on the sides with scenes from the saint's life, a gift of Queen Elizabeth of Austria, wife of Casimir the Jagiellon, in 1504. Produced by the Cracow goldsmith Marcin Marciniec. Gold, precious stones, height 24.3 cm, diagonal of the base 30.6 cm

Cathedral. Cathedral Treasury.
Detail of Piotr Kmita's chasuble
with its embroidered scenes from
the life of St. Stanislaus

Cathedral. Cathedral Treasury.
Gold Rose, a gift of Pope Clement
XII to Queen Maria Josepha, wife
of Augustus III

◄ Cathedral. Cathedral Treasury.
Royal crown dating from the 14th
century discovered at Sandomierz

◄ Cathedral. Cathedral Treasury.
Chasuble embroidered with pearls,
a gift of Cracow Voivode Piotr
Kmita, made in Cracow in circa
1504

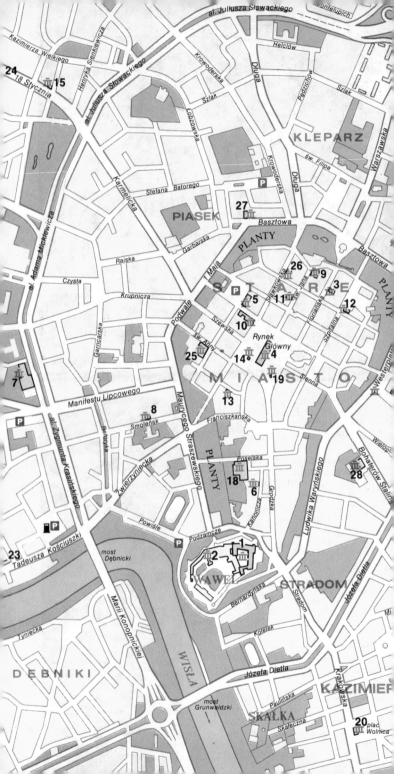

MUSEUMS

Cracow has as many as 28 museums and two more will soon be opened. The oldest of them, the Czartoryski Museum, was established in 1876, which by European standards is not so impressive perhaps, but we should remember that in the 19th century Poland was divided among three partitioning states and none of the invaders was particularly keen on collecting and displaying Polish national mementos and Polish art.

When in the aftermath of the partitions of Poland there was no longer the main patron of the arts, the royal court, the enlightened sections of society, who loved their country and traditions, tried to extend their protection to Polish art by establishing an appropriate institution. In Cracow the tradition of such activity goes back to the early 19th century.

These efforts came to fruition only in 1854 when Poland's first Society of the Friends of the Fine Arts was set up with the task of "awakening love of real and fundamental art"

---

1. State Art Collections at Wawel; 2. Cathedral Museum; 3. National Museum; 4. Painting Gallery in the Cloth Hall; 5. Szołayski House; 6. Stanisław Wyspiański Museum; 7. New Building; 8. Tapestry Display; 9. Czartoryski Collections; 10. Historical Museum of the City of Cracow; 11. Military Collections and Display of Clocks; 12. History of the Cracow Theatre; 13. Robert Jahoda's Printing and Book-binding Press; 14. Town Hall Tower; 15. Museum of Struggle and Martyrdom of the Poles; 16. History and Culture of Cracow Jewry; 17. Museum of National Remembrance in the "Eagle" Pharmacy; 18. Archaeological Museum; 19. Cellars of St. Adalbert's Church; 20. Ethnographic Museum; 21. Museum of Aviation and Aeronautics; 22. Lenin Museum; 23. Lenin's Home; 24. Rydlówka; 25. Museum of the Jagiellonian University; 26. Natural History Museum of the Polish Academy of Sciences; 27. Museum of Pharmacy of the Medical Academy; 28. Museum of the History of Photography

and "providing artists with the means of exhibiting and selling their work and supporting and encouraging the local artists to make greater advances in their art". The Society set about purchasing works of art with a view to handing them over to a future public museum. There were many private collections at the time, above all those belonging to more enlightened aristocratic families, such as the Czartoryskis in Puławy, the Ossolińskis and the Lubomirskis in Lvov, the Działyńskis and the Zamoyskis in Kórnik, and the Potockis at Wilanów in Warsaw. These collections however had no major bearing on the taste of society as a whole since they were not accessible to the general public.

THE NATIONAL MUSEUM (3)

During the last thirty years of the 19th century Cracow was the main centre of Polish culture, art and learning. When Prince Władysław Czartoryski brought to Cracow his collections, archives and library, the municipal authorities made available to him for their exhibition the Municipal Arsenal, the Carpenters' and Joiners' Towers and a small monastery at Pijarska Street, opposite the Czartoryski mansion. All these buildings were adapted to suit museum purposes and, joined by a Romantic arch with the mansion, turned this area into a charming corner of old Cracow.

The opening of the restored Cloth Hall in 1879 was combined with the celebrations of the 50th anniversary of work of the novelist Józef Ignacy Kraszewski. In the grand halls on the first floor of the Cloth Hall, gifts were deposited, tributes paid, speeches read and greetings exchanged, and the author was decorated with the Commander's Grand Cross of the Order of Francis Joseph. All this lasted for three days. In the Victoria restaurant at św. Anny Street, during a special dinner to which a hundred people were invited, the painter Henryk Siemiradzki offered to the mayor of Cracow, Dr. Mikołaj Zyblikiewicz, his largest and most famous canvas, *The Torches of Christianity* (also known as *Nero's Torches*). That was the beginning of a

public museum in the Cloth Hall. On the mayor's recom-
mendations, news of such a magnificent gift was made
public through posters displayed all over the town. Siemiradzki's gift was followed by donations from others. Such
were the origins of the first Polish National Museum
established by a special decree of the Municipal Council
which took it upon itself to support this institution. The
manager of the National Museum was Professor Władysław
Łuszczkiewicz, an outstanding historian of art, student of
the history of Cracow, and a well-known painter.

There were long debates on the name of the museum.
Finally it was given the name "national", for it was a
municipal, and thus not state or Austrian museum, and
moreover dedicated to Polish national art and aimed at
serving the Polish nation.

It soon became apparent that the public needed
museums, for until the outbreak of the First World War

New Building of the National Museum at no. 1, 3 Maja Street. Its
construction began in 1934 according to a design by Czesław
Boratyński. Bolesław Schmidt and Edward Kreisler

Lady with Ermine, by Leonardo da Vinci, circa 1485, oil on walnut wood, 54.4 by 39.3 cm. Czartoryski Collections of the National Museum

Landscape with the Good Samaritan, by Rembrandt, 1638, oil on oak wood, 46.5 by 66 cm. Czartoryski Collections of the National Museum

The Beautiful Madonna of Krużlowa, by an unknown artist, circa 1400, polychromed linden wood, height 118 cm. Szołayski Gallery of the National Museum

Detail of the
stained-glass window
showing St. Mary
Magdalene from the
Dominican church in
Cracow, first quarter of
the 15th century. New
Building of the National
Museum

Annuciation, by Master
Jerzy of Cracow, 1517,
tempera on wood, 145
by 104 cm. Czartoryski
Collections of the
National Museum

Portrait of the Jagiellon Family, by Lucas Cranach the Younger, circa 1554, oil on copper sheet. Czartoryski Collections of the National Museum

Bona Sforza, wife of King Sigismund the Old, from the studio of Lukas Cranach the Younger, circa 1554, oil on copper sheet, 19.7 by 17.8 cm. Czartoryski Collections of the National Museum

more than a dozen were established, six of them open to the general public. By 1900 the collections of the National Museum, amassed through purchases, donations and bequests, numbered up to 10,000 items.

Another important event in the development of the museum movement in Poland came in the 1930's with the opening of a large permanent exhibition in Wawel Castle which immediately became the most popular museum in

Coopers, by the Master of the Behem Codex, miniature in the *Codex picturatus Balthasaris Behem*, 1505, parchment, 14 by 14 cm. Jagiellonian Library

Battle of Vienna, detail of the painting showing King John III (Sobieski) during the final stage of the battle, by an unknown, probably Polish painter, late 17th century. Oil on canvas, 130 by 195 cm. Czartoryski Collections of the National Museum

Poland visited annually by millions of tourists. It has been in operation ever since though now it bears the name of the Wawel State Art Collections.

Augural shield of King John III (Sobieski), Milan (?), mid-16th century. Metal, diameter 70 cm, weight 4.09 kg. Czartoryski Collections of the National Museum

Kontush sashes. I: Leon Madżarski's manufactory in Słuck, late 18th century, silk, silver thread, 35.5 by 362 cm. II: Antoni Puciłowski's manufactory in Cracow, second half of the 18th century, silk, gold and silver thread, 32 by 387 cm. Czartoryski Collections of the National Museum

Saddle that belonged to Prince Adam Kazimierz Czartoryski as commander of the Galician Gentry Guard. Polish workmanship, circa 1783, blue velvet embroidered in gold thread, gilded metal sheet studded with carnelians. Czartoryski Collections of the National Museum

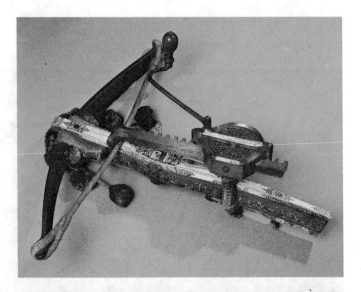

18th century hunting cross-bow with its crank and jack dating from 1537. Saxon workmanship probably made to a Polish order since it bears at the bottom the Sulima coat-of-arms. Wood, ivory engraved with hunting scenes, metal, bronze fittings. Length of the bar 42 cm, length of the entire cross-bow 69.5 cm, length of the bowstring 68 cm. Czartoryski Collections of the National Museum

China figures, Meissen, modelled on Johann Joachim Kändler's work, circa mid-18th century. Height 15.3 cm. Czartoryski Collections of the National Museum

The National Museum has retained its leading position among Polish museums. In 1945 it had as many as 300,000 exhibits. It has formed branches all over the city. The magnificent bequests of the Czapski family (the first of them in 1903 and the last in 1980) — coins and medals, books, old maps of Poland, etchings and old prints — form

Glassware
I: Corda Fidelium cup, Urzecze manufactory, second half of the 18th century, height 26.5 cm; II: cup, Urzecze manufactory, mid-18th century, height 20.6 cm; III: cup with the coats-of-arms of Michał Kazimierz Radziwiłł and his wife Urszula Franciszka née Wiśniowiecka, Urzecze or Naliboki manufactory, second quarter of the 18th century, height 40 cm; IV: cup with two helbard bearers and the inscription "Vivat dobre zdrowie Waszeci" (Vivat to your good health), unidentified Polish manufactory, circa 1700, height 20 cm; V: flute cup with the Topór coat-of-arms, Naliboki or Urzecze manufactory, early 19th century, height 29.5 cm
Czartoryski Collections of the National Museum in Cracow

Man with Parrot, by Józef Simmler, 1859, oil on canvas, 45 by 32 cm. Cloth Hall Gallery of the National Museum

a separate branch at Manifestu Lipcowego Street. Another branch is the house of the painter Jan Matejko, together with part of the artist's collection and numerous private donations. The third branch was formed thanks to a bequest by Adam and Włodzimiera Szołayski, which included their attractive mansion at the corner of Szczepański Square and Szczepańska Street, together with the splendid collections it contained. In 1920 an excellent collection, including objects of Japanese art, was bequeathed by Feliks Jasieński-Manggha. Since there was no

Ahasuerus (Self-portrait), by Maurycy Gottlieb, 1876, oil on canvas, 65 by 53 cm. Cloth Hall Gallery of the National Museum

Powiśle, by Aleksander Gierymski, 1883, oil on canvas, 64.5 by 47.5 cm. Cloth Hall Gallery of the National Museum

Death of Ellenai, by Jacek Malczewski, 1883, oil on canvas, 212 by 370 cm. Cloth Hall Gallery of the National Museum

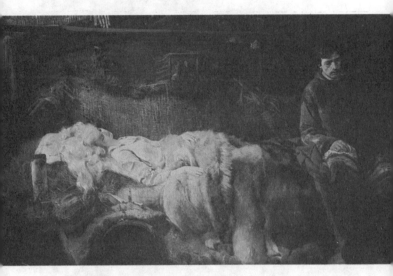

modern exhibition hall or administrative centre for the whole museum, in 1934 work began on the construction of a New Building, the first part of which was completed in 1939, while the rest is still under construction.

In 1950 the National Museum took over the Czartoryski Museum in trust and the Industrial Museum permanently. The former raised the prestige of the museum as an international centre of Polish culture, and that despite the fact that the Nazis had stolen many excellent works of art, including the mementos of the Polish kings, part of the collection of old gold jewellery and a dozen or so paintings, among them Raphael's *Portrait of a Young Man.*

At present the collections of the National Museum number 650,000 items of which a small part only is put on display. It boasts such masterpieces as Leonardo da Vinci's *Lady with an Ermine* and Rembrandt's *Landscape with the*

Ecstasy, by Władysław Podkowiński, 1894, oil on canvas, 310 by 275 cm. Cloth Hall Gallery of the National Museum

Temptation of St. Anthony, by Stanisław Ignacy Witkiewicz, 1916—21, tempera on canvas, 74.5 by 90 cm. Cloth Hall Gallery of the National Museum

Self-portrait with Wife, by Stanisław Wyspiański, 1904, pastel on cardboard, 47.5 by 62.2 cm. New Building of the National Museum

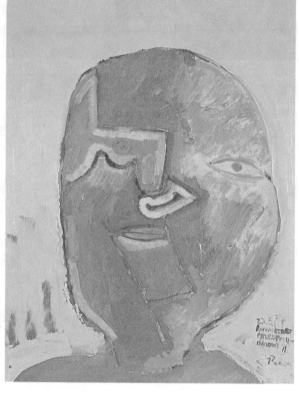

Still-life with Knife, by Józef Pankiewicz, 1909, oil on canvas, 52 by 65.5 cm. New Building of the National Museum

Morning Self-portrait II, by Jerzy Panek, 1972, oil on canvas, 81 by 65 cm. New Building of the National Museum

Pole 1979, by Leszek Sobocki, 1979, oil on hardboard, 90 by 90 cm. New Building of the National Museum

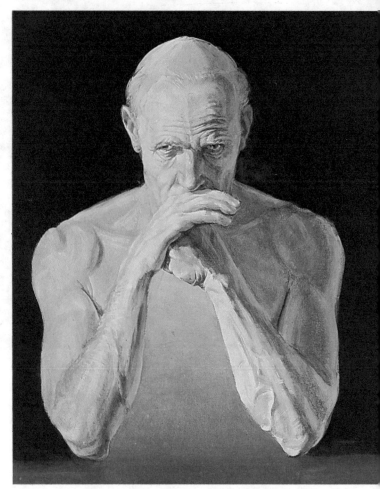

Portrait of Professor Leon Chwistek, by Stanisław Ignacy Witkiewicz,
1923, pastel on paper, 65 by 48 cm. Museum of the Jagiellonian
University

Good Samaritan, as well as Polish works ranging from those dating from the earliest times to the present day.

The National Museum has the following branches: the **Painting Gallery in the Cloth Hall** (4) (Polish painting and sculpture, 1764—1900); the **New Building** (7) (Polish painting and sculpture from the late 19th century to the present day); the **Hutten-Czapski Collection** (coins and medals, prints and maps; closed to the public); the **Czartoryski Collections** (9) (historical mementos and European painting); **Jan Matejko's House** (mementos of the artist, his paintings and drawings); the **Gallery in the Szołayski House** (5) (Polish painting and sculpture until 1765); the **Stanisław Wyspiański Museum** (6) (mementos of the artist, his publications and paintings); the **Czartoryski Library;** and the **Karol Szymanowski Museum** in the villa Atma in Zakopane (mementos of the composer).

THE HISTORICAL MUSEUM OF THE CITY OF CRACOW (10)

This museum was set up by a resolution of the Municipal Council of 1899. For several dozen years it was merely one of the small branches of the Archives of Old Documents. It was only in December 1945 that it became an independent institution the aim of which was to "collect and preserve all kinds of museum material that would illustrate the life and culture of the city of Cracow from the earliest times until today". Soon the Historical Museum became one of Cracow's major cultural institutions, with a collection of over 50,000 items displayed in seven branches.

The main building, in the Krzysztofory mansion in the Main Market Place, houses the section dealing with the **History and Culture of Cracow.** In view of Cracow's rich theatrical tradition (Cracow has Poland's oldest theatre building in existence for 200 years), a separate branch, in the 15th-century Under the Cross House in św. Ducha Square, is devoted to the **History of the Cracow Theatre** (12). The Renaissance synagogue in Kazimierz is occupied

by a display on the **History and Culture of Cracow Jewry**
(16). The Town Hall Tower contains an exhibition concern-
ed with the **History of the Municipal Authorities** (14). The
section of **Military Collections and Clocks** (11) is to be
found in the Krauze house at 12 św. Jana Street. The
former Gestapo headquarters in 2 Pomorska Street, where
thousands of Poles were tortured to death, has been turned
into a **Museum of Struggle and Martyrdom of the Poles**
(15). And finally, at 4 Gołębia Street, in the premises of the
well-known firm of the Jahodas, you may visit **Robert
Jahoda's Printing and Book-binding Press** (13) with a
display dealing with the history of printing and book-
binding.

THE ARCHAEOLOGICAL MUSEUM (18)

In 1850 the Cracow Learned Society that was established
in 1816 set up a Museum of Antiquity and soon, in answer
to an appeal issued by the Society, interesting finds began
to flow in, including a stone figure of Światowid, a Slavonic
deity, dating from the late 7th and early 8th centuries, that
had been discovered in 1848 in the Zbruch river.

Excavation work carried out in the area of Cracow has
yielded many valuable finds that show the development of
material culture in this region. East of Cracow, for example,
potters' kilns dating from the Roman period were found,
one of them crammed with 92 excellently fired pots.

Before the construction of Poland's largest foundry, the
Lenin metallurgical combine, began in 1950, the site had
been carefully examined by archaeologists from the
museum. Many pre-historic and early-mediaeval objects
were unearthed and a special branch of the museum was
opened in Nowa Huta.

The museum carries out large-scale research on ancient
iron smelting in the Świętokrzyskie (Holy Cross) Moun-
tains. It also keeps a close check on all excavation work in
the Cracow area. On one such occasion traces of an ancient
iron works were discovered in the area of the Main Market

Place (by the Under the Rams Mansion). On another occasion, in 1979, a treasure trove containing 3,800 pre-monetary tokens of exchange, weighing four tons and dating from the late 8th and early 9th centuries, was found in the cellar of an annex to the house at 13 Kanonicza Street.

In 1967 the Archaeological Museum moved to its present premises in a group of former monastery buildings dating from the 17th century (entrance from Poselska Street). Centuries ago this site was occupied by the so-called Painted Manor House of the voivodes Tęczyński. Later it was taken over by Discalced Carmelites, followed by the Austrians who turned the monastery into the St. Michael prison where later, during the Second World War, many Poles perished.

The museum collections are divided into four permanent exhibitions: **Mediterranean Archaeology;** the **Ancient History and Middle Ages of Little Poland;** the **Early History of Nowa Huta,** and the **History of the Former St. Michael Prison.** The museum has a branch in the basement of St. Adalbert's Church in the Main Market Place, with a display devoted to the **History of the Cracow Main Market Place** (19), featuring such objects as wooden sewage and water mains, ornaments and vessels discovered by archaeologists during the general renovation of the surface of the Market Place carried out in 1962—63.

THE ETHNOGRAPHIC MUSEUM (20)

Cracow evinced an interest in folk culture a long time ago. In the 19th century such institutions as the Museum of Technology and Industry, the Jagiellonian University, the Academy of Learning, the Polish Applied Art Society and the National Museum started collecting objects connected with folklore and folk art. The decision to establish an ethnographic museum in Cracow was taken in 1901, owing to which we now have Poland's oldest museum of this kind.

For many years the museum did not have its own

building and developed haphazardly. But in 1947 it was given the old town hall (its present Renaissance form dating from the 16th century) of Kazimierz and since then it has considerably expanded its collections which today number 61,000 items displayed in three basic sections: **Polish Culture from the Area of All Poland and the Former Commonwealth of Poland; European Folk Culture,** mostly the culture of the Slavonic peoples; **Non-European Folk Culture from Asia, America, Oceania and Africa.** In addition the museum has its own archives with a collection of 100,000 items, including manuscripts, drawings, recordings, films and slides, as well as many valuable publications by most outstanding Polish ethnographers, such as Józef Lompa, Oskar Kolberg, Seweryn Udziela, Kazimierz Moszyński and Tadeusz Seweryn.

THE LENIN MUSEUM (22)

The Lenin Museum, opened in 1954, occupies an attractive neo-classicist mansion at 5 Topolowa Street, not far from those places where Lenin, the future leader of the Russian Revolution, stayed in 1912—14. The museum has on display many original documents, decrees and newspapers from those years. Lenin's first apartment in Cracow, at 41 Królowej Jadwigi Street, has been turned into a branch of the museum, **Lenin's Home** (23). South of Cracow you can visit two other branches of the same museum, at **Biały Dunajec** and at **Poronin,** where Lenin spent his holidays and held meetings. Also preserved has been the cell in the former prison in Nowy Targ (at present a Youth Club) where Lenin was kept after his arrest by the Austrians in August 1914.

THE MUSEUM OF AVIATION AND AERONAUTICS (21)

Though this museum was set up in 1963, the Cracow Aeroclub had started collecting exhibits much earlier. You can see original aircraft and engines dating from before the First World War. It was not by chance that the museum was established in Cracow, for it was in this city that in April 1910 the first Polish aircraft was built. The museum also boasts the only surviving Polish P 11-C fighter plane. As regard the number of exhibits, the museum is the 10th largest in the world and 6th largest in Europe.

*

There are many more museums in Cracow and each of them deserves a visit. For detailed information on addresses and opening hours, see pp. 191—195.

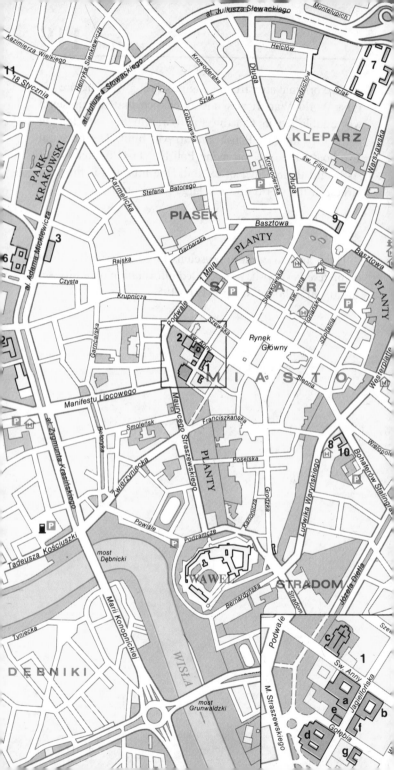

THE COLLEGIUM MAIUS AND THE UNIVERSITY QUARTER

On 12 May 1364 King Casimir the Great established the first university in Poland, which after Prague was the second university in Central Europe. Restored in 1400 by King Ladislaus Jagiello it has conducted lively research and teaching activity ever since. It was known in all of Europe and its various courses were attended by many prominent representatives of Polish science and learning, culture and politics. The most famous student to attend the university was Nicolaus Copernicus (Mikołaj Kopernik) who studied here in the years 1491—95.

It is still a mystery where the university had its first headquarters, at Wawel Hill or in the vicinity of the town hall at Kazimierz. In the year 1400, thanks to a bequest by Queen Jadwiga, King Ladislaus Jagiello purchased for 600 *grzywnas* a square and houses at the corner of the present św. Anny and Jagiellońska Streets for the needs of the Cracow Academy. Lectures began on 24 July 1400. At first the university had three faculties — law, medicine and philosophy — and a fourth, theology, was added soon. The reputation that the university enjoyed attracted many foreigners who in the 15th century constituted almost half of the whole student body. The conditions in the original building began to be cramped and in the 15th century the academy was rebuilt and expanded. A new building with an

1. Jagiellonian University: a. Collegium Maius; b. Kołłątaj College; c. Academic Church of St. Anne; d. Collegium Novum; e. Collegium Minus; f. Collegium Physicum; g. Collegium Slavisticum; 2. Medical Academy (the Rector's Office in the Nowodworski College); 3. Agricultural Academy; 4. Physical Education Academy; 5. Academy of Economics; 6. Academy of Mining and Metallurgy; 7. Cracow Polytechnic; 8. Academy of Music; 9. Academy of Fine Arts; 10. Higher State Drama College; 11. Teachers' Training College; 12. Jagiellonian Library

arcaded courtyard was erected, with lecture rooms on the ground floor and the professors' rooms upstairs.

In the 16th century, the era of the Renaissance, which was conducive to the development of learning, as many as 9,600 students attended various university courses. During the Counter-Reformation period the Jesuits established in Cracow a rival higher education institution and although the university continued to hold the position of pre-eminence, the standards of scholarship deteriorated and the academy was threatened with decline.

In 1773, during the Enlightenment period, a Commission for National Education, Europe's first ministry of education, was established in Poland. The new rector of the Jagiellonian University, Father Hugo Kołłątaj, carried out a number of reforms that transformed the college into a modern higher education institution that attracted outstanding scholars from all over Poland. At the time the university acquired modern laboratories, clinics, a botanical garden and an astronomical observatory. Various experiments were carried out, for example in January 1784, the first Polish hot air balloon was launched.

The hardest period in the over 600 years long history of the university came during the Nazi occupation. On 6 November 1939, apparently on the occasion of the beginning of the new academic year, the Germans invited the majority of the university's academic staff, as well as some from the Mining Academy, to an academic conference. A hundred and eighty-three professors arrived. They were first brutally beaten up and then dispatched to concentration camps where thirty of them perished. The university was officially closed down although despite the terror unleashed by the invader it continued operating secretly. Each day clandestine lectures and classes were held in private homes, exams were taken and scholarly papers written. These underground classes were attended by a total of 800 students.

The custom of preserving various scientific and historical objects of the university goes back to the 15th century. The university collection was expanded with gifts from Queen Jadwiga, Duchess Alexandra of Mazovia, Cardinal Zbigniew Oleśnicki, Cardinal Frederick the Jagiellon, successive kings, representatives of aristocratic families and professors. For example in 1492, Marcin Bylica of Olkusz presented a collection of astronomical instruments. The most valuable objects were, and still are, kept in the treasury of the Collegium Maius.

In the 19th century the collection was separated from the Library. The Austrian authorities did not like the use of the word museum, and therefore the collection was referred to as the Cabinet of Art and Archaeology. In the years 1886—1940 it was accommodated in the Collegium Novum. After the Second World War part of the collection which had been looted by the Germans returned to Cracow, but the rest was irretrievably lost, including Wit Stwosz's drawings and letters. The museum obtained new premises in the Collegium Maius which in 1949—64 was thoroughly reconstructed. The **Collegium Maius** (56) is a fine example of 15th century Gothic architecture. Its façade facing Jagiellońska Street has an oriel window and the inner courtyard, surrounded by 15th century arcades, features a staircase leading from the ground floor — where lecture rooms are to be found — to the first floor with its halls for official ceremonies. The former Stuba Communis is where new university rectors are elected, academic meetings held and particularly important visitors received.

Legend has it that in the Alchemy Hall two 16th century alchemists, Faustus and Pan Twardowski, conducted their experiments, while it is a fact that in the lecture room next to it, Nicolaus Copernicus studied. The treasury on the first floor contains a collection of rector's maces, globes and clocks, as well as Poland's oldest soldier's uniform, excellently preserved, together with a cartridge pouch, dating from 1770. The owner of this uniform was a participant in the Confederacy of Bar, the standard bearer of the Sącz county and volunteer in the Kosciuszko insurrection, Romuald Prus Lisiecki. In the Stuba Communis you may admire a complete set of pewter and copper vessels. The overdoor of the Renaissance portal of this hall is emblazoned with the device of the university: *Plus ratio quam vis* (Reason [means] more than force).

The Jagiellonian University has six science museums: the Jagiellonian University Museum, the Zoologicial Museum, the origins of which go back to the 18th century, the Geological and Mineralogical Museums also dating from the 18th century, the Anthropological Museum, and the Print Room in the Jagiellonian Library (The Museum of the History of Medicine belongs at present to the Medical Academy). Naturally enough these 18th century museums are collections of teaching and scientific aids rather than museums as we understand the word today.

The Jagiellonian Library is one of the largest libraries in Poland with its collection of almost three million volumes, including 3,248 incunabula and 100,000 old prints. Its prize items are the *Codex of Balthasar Behem* dating from 1505 and a register of students beginning in the 15th century. In the latter, in the winter semester of 1491, we can see a note concerning Copernicus, saying *Nicolaus Nicolai de Thuronia solvit totum* (Nicolaus son of Nicolaus of Toruń paid the whole sum). The Library also boasts a record of the popular hymn of the Polish knights, *Bogurodzica* (Mother of God) from 1407 and the original manuscript of Copernicus' *De revolutionibus orbium coelestium* published in 1543.

The part of the Old Town where the Collegium Maius is situated is also referred to as the university quarter since most of the buildings here belong or used to belong to the university. Next to the Collegium Maius, at 6 św. Anny Street, stands the **Kołłątaj College** (57), formerly known as the Collegium Physicum. The **Nowodworski College** at no. 12 (58) used to be what was once Poland's oldest lycée preparing pupils to take up studies at the Jagiellonian University. Established in 1586, today it is a secondary school in new and better premises at Na Groblach Square and it is still closely associated with the university. Its old building dating from 1639—43 is the main administrative building of the Medical Academy.

St. Anne's Church (hence the name of the street, św. Anny) opposite (59) has been for centuries a university church. This beautiful Baroque edifice was built in 1689—1705 according to a design by Tylman van Gameren as the third church on this site where the first Gothic church had burnt down in 1407. The stuccos inside the church are the work of Balthasar Fontana. Among the many gravestones and epitaphs dedicated to professors of the university, there is a monument of Nicolaus Copernicus which on its base

Façade of the Collegium Maius with its oldest, stone, part dating from the 14th century, the gable from 1507 and the buttress from the 18th century

bears the inscription *Sapere auso* (To the one who dared to be sapient).

A stone's throw from here, next to the **Collegium Novum** (60) amidst greenery by the Planty park, you will come across the **Copernicus statue** (61) sculpted in 1900 by Cyprian Godebski, who showed the great astronomer as a scholar of the Cracow academy.

Gołębia Street running parallel to św. Anny Street is also lined by university buildings: the **Collegium Minus** (62) at no. 11, the **Collegium Physicum** at no. 13 (63) and the **Collegium Slavisticum** at no. 20 (64).

Arcaded courtyard (circa 1493) of the Collegium Maius were various ceremonies and theatre performances where held and students rested in between classes. Built by the architect Johannes of Cologne

Aula of the Collegium Maius called the Jagiellonian Hall where on 22 June 1983 Pope John Paul II, who years before had studied Polish and theology at the Jagiellonian University, received an honorary doctorate

The treasury of the Museum of the Jagiellonian University in the Collegium Maius contains, among other items, rector's sceptres. In the photo: the world's oldest university sceptre dating from the late 14th century, a gift of Queen Jadwiga. Gilded silver, length 110.6 cm. The other sceptre dates from 1454 and was a gift of Cardinal Zbigniew Oleśnicki. Gilded silver, length 115.9 cm

Jagiellonian Globe or a clock with the so-called armillary sphere, which enjoys deserved fame due to the fact that the American continent is marked on it with the inscription *America noviter reperta*. Circa 1510, diameter of the globe 7.3 cm, together with the sphere 12 cm

In his *Weltchronik* the German geographer Hartmann Schedel wrote the following in 1493: "Cracow has a famous university, rich in many brilliant and very learned men where numerous liberal arts are taught. However astronomy stands highest among them. And in the whole of Germany there is no more famous university as we well know from stories told by many."

For over 600 years the Jagiellonian University has set the tone for Cracow and for Polish scholarship. As in the past, today too young people from many countries attend its various courses. And for years too the beautiful Collegium Maius, and the Jagiellonian University Museum, have attracted crowds of tourists and have taught them the history of this oldest university in Poland.

Since 1945 the university has expanded considerably and many of its faculties have acquired the status of independent institutions of higher education, for example the Nicolaus Copernicus Medical Academy, the Hugo Kołłątaj Agricultural Academy, the Bronisław Czech Physical Ed-

Picture showing the most famous student of the Jagiellonian University, Nicolaus Copernicus, in the aula of the Collegium Novum, painted by Jan Matejko, 1873. Oil on canvas, 225 by 315 cm

Statue of Nicolaus Copernicus as a student in the Planty park next to the Collegium Novum, sculpted by Cyprian Godebski, bronze, 1900

ucation Academy and the Academy of Economics. Besides, there are also a number of technical universities, such as the Stanisław Staszic Mining and Metallurgical Academy, the Tadeusz Kosciuszko Polytechnic, and the Stanisław Ziaja Officers' College, as well as the Academy of Music, the Jan Matejko Academy of Fine Arts, the Ludwik Solski Higher State Drama College, and the Teachers' Training College named after the Commission for National Education. Finally Cracow boasts the Papal Theological Academy, many scientific institutes and many branches of the Polish Academy of Sciences. In all some 50,000 students study here and 23,000 people are associated with science, including 7,500 academic staff, which makes Cracow Poland's second largest academic centre after Warsaw.

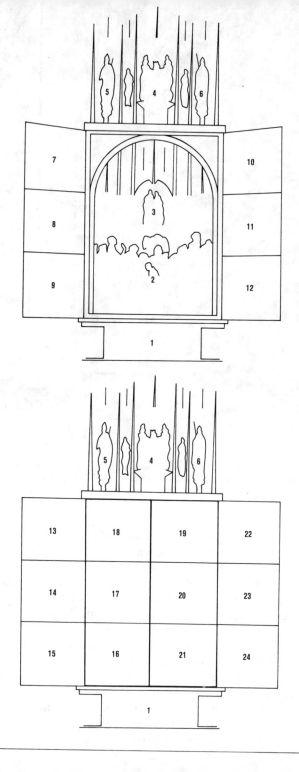

WIT STWOSZ AND ST. MARY'S CHURCH

The gem of the Main Market Place is the archpresbyterial church dedicated to the Assumption of the Blessed Virgin Mary, popularly referred to as St. Mary's or the Marian Church, its bulk dominating the Market Place and the entire Old Town. It was always a parish church under special protection of the Cracow burghers of whom the most powerful and wealthiest patrician families — the Wierzyneks, the Boners, the Montelupis, the Salomons and the Cellaris — had their own chapels here.

The first Romanesque church was built on this site in the years 1222—23, before the laying out of the Main Market Place in 1257. This church was oriented (the chancel was in the east) and therefore its front stands at an angle in relation to the later regular arrangement of the streets. The builders who were employed on its construction in 1290—1300 made partial use of the foundations and walls of the first church. The present form of the church dates from 1392—97 and was the work of Mikołaj Werner who turned the old hall structure into a basilica with a nave and two aisles. In the years 1400—06 the towers were completed and

---

Open altar: 1. Predella with the Tree of Jesse; 2. Dormition of the Virgin Mary; 3. Assumption of the Virgin Mary; 4. Coronation of the Virgin Mary; 5. Saint Stanislaus; 6. Saint Adalbert; 7. Annunciation of the Virgin Mary; 8. Nativity; 9. Adoration of the Magi; 10. Resurrection; 11. Ascension; 12. Descent of the Holy Ghost. **Closed altar:** 1. Predella with the Tree of Jesse; 4. Coronation of the Virgin Mary; 5. Saint Stanislaus; 6. Saint Adalbert; 13. Meeting of Saint Joachim and Saint Anne; 14. Birth of Mary; 15. Presentation of Mary in the Temple; 16. Presentation of Christ in the Temple; 17. Infant Jesus teaching in the Temple; 18. Arrest; 19. Crucifixion; 20. Deposition; 21. Entombment; 22. Christ in Limbo; 23. Three Marys at the Sepulchre; 24. Christ and Saint Mary Magdalene.

in 1478 the higher spire acquired a dome with a pinnacle surrounded by turrets. The crown dates from the 17th century. The higher spire (81 metres) is a municipal guard tower from which you can hear the bugle call that is known to all Poles — since at noon it is broadcast throughout the country as a time signal. The lower spire (69 metres), topped with a 16th century Renaissance dome, is a bell tower and contains the Demi-Sigismund bell dating from 1438, which, as legend has it, was carried to the top of the tower by the young magnate Stanisław Ciołek who was famed for his exceptional strength.

There are four entrances to the church: the main entrance from the Market Place, the southern and northern doors and the fourth entrance leading to the chancel only. By the southern entrance from Mariacki Square you can see mediaeval iron stocks once used to punish criminals and the ill-mannered, for example traders who screamed abuse at their customers. In the gallilee of the main entrance, there are two 14th century fonts on each side.

The nave, rising to the height of 28 metres, has Gothic vaulting. Beyond the rood-screen lies the chancel where your eye is caught by Wit Stwosz's Marian altar glittering with gold and the colours of the spectrum. However before we reach the high altar, let us take a look at the rest of the interior.

First there are magnificent polychrome paintings by Jan Matejko the colours of which perfectly harmonize with the light from the mediaeval stained-glass windows in the chancel, the gilded altar-piece and the stained-glass windows designed by Stanisław Wyspiański and Józef Mehoffer for the area above the choir loft.

Among the many objects of Gothic, Renaissance and Baroque art, two crucifixes deserve particular attention: one displayed on the rood-screen between the nave and the chancel, which is the work of a pupil of Wit Stwosz dating from circa 1520, and the other, the work of Wit Stwosz, endowed in 1491 by Henryk Slacker, the master of the royal mint, which is to be seen in the last altar of the right aisle.

Right by the rood-screen you will see late Renaissance (circa 1600) two-tiered sarcophagi of the Montelupi and Cellari families. The pillars of the nave are adorned with fine paintings by Hans Süss von Kulmbach dating from the early 16th century. The chapels surrounding the church, which were endowed by rich guilds or wealthy patricians, contain a large quantity of works of art: tomb stones, commemorative plaques, altar-pieces and bronze gratings. The stalls in the chancel constitute a fine example of Cracow Baroque wood-carving (after 1620), and the Renaissance ciborium, dating from 1555, is the work of Gianmaria Padovano who also rebuilt the Cloth Hall.

St. Mary's Church has its own treasury, entered through the chancel. It contains Gothic chalices, monstrances, reliquaries, pyxes, crosses, candle-holders and a collection of liturgical vestments which is the best in Poland in terms of quantity (300 chasubles alone, some of them dating from the Gothic era) and age.

The chancel, illuminated by mediaeval (1370—90) stained-glass windows, is dominated by a grand altar-piece, the work of Wit Stwosz, one of the finest masterpieces of European late-mediaeval wood-carving, thought to be the largest wooden Gothic altar-piece in Europe. Its author was born in 1448 in the town of Horb on the Neckar in Swabia. His surname was variously spelled as Schtoss, Stwoss, Stwosz, Stvos, Stosche and Stosz, as was his first name which has come down to us as Vit, Fit, Vitus, Feyt and Vaydt. He arrived in Cracow from Nuremberg in 1477, and here he spent the twenty best years of his life before he returned to Nuremberg where he died in the autumn of 1533.

He began his magnum opus on 25 May 1477. When six years later the Cracow councillors saw what he had done so far, they were so impressed that they released the master from the duty of paying the municipal tax. After twelve years Wit Stwosz completed his work in July 1489.

During the Second World War the Nazis took the Marian altar to the Reich and kept it hidden there in

The Nativity Scene (The Adoration of the Shepherds), panel in the inner wings of Wit Stwosz's altar-piece

High Altar in St. Mary's Church carved in wood by Wit Stwosz, 1477—89

various places. Found after the war, it returned to Cracow in 1946 in very poor condition whereupon it had to be meticulously restored until in 1957 it returned to the church where it was installed with the help of the same windlass that Wit Stwosz had used in 1489. This old windlass is still to be seen in the attic over the chancel, right above the altar-piece.

The altar is a pentaptych: a large altar cabinet and four wings, two of them movable and two immovable. Its base is a predella (the part of the altar that rests on the mensa) with the Tree of Jesse, or the Virgin Mary's genealogical tree. The predella is modelled on a drawing by the Netherlandish artist, Israel van Mackenem.

With the altar closed you see twelve bas-relief panels which, viewed from left to right from the top, show scenes from the life of the Madonna and Christ.

When the wings are open, the interior of the altar cabinet is revealed with the central scene representing the Dormition and the Assumption of the Virgin Mary. The Dormition is a reference to *The Golden Legend* (*Legenda aurea*) according to which the Madonna died peacefully surrounded by the apostles. This central scene is encircled by figures of prophets and patriarchs and, in the top corners, the Fathers of the Church, St. St. Gregory, Jerome, Ambrose and Augustine.

The side wings, from the top left looking down, represent the Annunciation, the Nativity, the Adoration of the Magi and, on the right, the Resurrection, the Ascension and the Descent of the Holy Ghost.

The altar is topped by the Coronation of the Madonna and figures of the patron saints of Poland, Stanislaus on the left hand side and Adalbert on the right.

When open, the altar is 11 metres wide and its height is 12.85 metres. The cabinet is 5.34 metres wide and together with the wings, 7.25 metres high. The tallest figures are 2.8 metres high and weigh several hundred kilograms. To produce his masterpiece Wit Stwosz used three kinds of. wood: oak of which the load bearing elements are made;

larch, to plank the whole altar; and linden from which he sculpted over 200 figures and almost 2,000 details, finials, tracery, arches, etc. Large heavy trunks of 500 year old linden trees were floated up the Vistula to Cracow from the nearby Niepołomice Forest.

The Marian altar is truly the magnum opus of Wit Stwosz but also of the city of Cracow, for it provides a picture of mediaeval Cracow and shows its everyday life. When we look closely at the individual panels, we can learn a lot about the inhabitants of Old Cracow, how different classes dressed, what arms they wielded, what diseases they suffered from, what kind of furniture and what pots and pans they used. We also know or rather we can guess what Wit Stwosz looked like: in the right hand corner of the Crucifixion panel, you can see a figure of a man in rich attire lost in thought. It is said that this is how Wit Stwosz represented himself.

KAZIMIERZ

Once a town in its own right, established in 1335, Kazimierz got its name after its founder, King Casimir the Great. Not all that long ago it was separated from Cracow by the village of Stradom and the Stara Wisła, an arm of the Vistula, which in the second half of the 19th century was filled with earth and in its place a street was laid out, named in honour of Józef Dietl, Mayor of Cracow in 1866—74.

The village of Stradom, known as early as 1378, was relatively quickly, in 1415, administratively incorporated into Kazimierz, and together with the latter became part of Cracow only in 1800. Although Stradom was an autonomous village for a short time only and for centuries constituted a part of Kazimierz and later of Cracow, nevertheless its old name — rather unusual, perhaps coming from the Italian *strada?* — has been preserved and continues to be in general use.

After a bridge had been built over the Vistula in 1802, Stradom gained in importance. It had its staging post and new hotels, inns, bath-houses, a customs house and other facilities. On his way through Cracow, Honoré de Balzac stopped at the White Rose Hotel in Stradom.

At present Stradom boasts two major tourist sights: the **Bernardine church and monastery** (1) and the **church of the Missionary Fathers** (2). In 1450, envoys of King Casimir the

---

1. Bernardine church and monastery; 2. Church and monastery of the Missionary Fathers; 3. Church and monastery of the Brothers of the Order of St. John of God; 4. Church of St. Catherine; 5. Pauline church and monastery on the Cliff; 6. Town Hall (Ethnographic Museum); 7. Corpus Christi Church; 8. Old Synagogue; 9. Rema Synagogue; 10. Poper Synagogue; 11. Ajzyk Synagogue; 12. High Synagogue; 13. Kupa Synagogue; 14. Reformed (Tempel) Synagogue

Jagiellon brought from Wrocław the famous Italian preacher Giovanni Capistrano (later St. John Capistrano) who preached so convincingly in the Market Place that the sinful Cracovians fetched from their homes various valuable objects which were burnt in the square. They also began in large numbers to join the Bernardine order, established in 1453 and following the rule of St. Francis. In 1454 Cardinal Zbigniew Oleśnicki had a church built which in 1655 during the Swedish invasion was destroyed by the Swedish army which besieged Cracow. Restored in 1680 in Baroque style the church contains many paintings and sculptures. The chapel of St. Anne features a figure of St. Anne with the Madonna and Child, ascribed to Wit Stwosz. In the left aisle you will see a 17th century painted representation of the Danse Macabre. The sacristy holds the reliquary of the Blessed Simon of Lipnica whose tomb is to be seen in a chapel on the right side of the church. Beyond the church and the monastery there are beautiful gardens which once reached as far as the Vistula.

The Missionary Fathers, who were invited to Poland by Queen Marie Louise in 1651, appeared in Cracow in 1682. A church and monastery were built for them at no. 4 Stradom Street between 1719 and 1732. Although its façade has never been completed it is still regarded as one of the finest Baroque churches in Cracow. Inside, you can admire paintings by Tadeusz Konicz known in Rome where he later worked as Taddeo Polacco, dating from the 18th century and a portrait of King Stephen Báthory by the royal painter Marcin Kober of Wrocław.

STRADOM comes to an end when it joins DIETLA STREET, on the other side of which it becomes KRAKOWSKA STREET situated in Kazimierz. The founder of the town of Kazimierz endowed it generously: he assigned to it a vast area (900 by 500 metres) in the fork of the Vistula (the main bed and the Stara Wisła), encircled it with walls with seven gates, laid out a market square, initiated the construction of two large churches, of St. Catherine and Corpus Christi, and a town hall, granted various privileges to the local merchants and craftsmen, and in 1364 began the building of a university. Unfortunately he died before he had a chance to complete his grand project.

When in the 15th century plans were drawn up to build a university at the corner of Jagiellońska and św. Anny Streets, Jews living in this part of Cracow were removed to the area of today's Szczepański Square and Sławkowska Street, but they were not destined to stay there for long since in 1495 King John Albert had them resettled outside Cracow, to Kazimierz, where in time a large Jewish community, called the Jewish Town, arose, governed by their own laws and customs. Jews built here their synagogues, schools, printing houses and cemeteries. The town was divided by a wall into two parts, Jewish Kazimierz and Christian Kazimierz.

We shall begin our sightseeing tour of Kazimierz, today a district of Old Cracow, at KRAKOWSKA STREET which is a continuation of the route leading from Floriań-ska, across the Main Market Place, Grodzka, Wawel and Stradom. Though mentioned in old records as early as 1385, Krakowska Street is lined mostly by 19th century houses. In its further section to the left, there are the **church and monastery of the Brothers of the Order of St. John of God,** (3), formerly of the Trinitarians. The late Baroque church (1741—58) has a fine façade and inside illusionistic polychrome paintings. In the years 1870—95, the outstanding ethnographer, professor at the Jagiellonian University, Żegota Pauli, lived in the monastery. Opposite the church, at no. 43, there is a workhouse established by the Blessed Brother Albert (Adam Chmielowski), the founder of the congregation of the Albertine Brothers.

Taking SKAŁECZNA STREET to the right we reach one of Cracow's most picturesque corners. First, there is the **Church of St. Catherine** (4) which is joined by an arch with the Augustine convent. At a distance you can see the towers and the façade of the Pauline Church on the Cliff. The Church of St. Catherine was endowed by King Casimir the Great in 1363 for the Augustine order brought from Prague. Its construction took a long time and was completed in 1400, and now it is regarded as one of the finest Gothic structures in Poland. The gallilee, sumptuously lined with stone, was built in the early 15th century. The beautiful monastery cloisters feature invaluable Gothic paintings while in a small square chapel, the vaulting of

Pauline church and monastery on the Cliff. The church is associated with the history of Bishop St. Stanislaus who in 1079 was condemned to death by King Boleslaus the Bold, following which each successive king of Poland on ascending the throne was obliged to make a penitential pilgrimage from the castle to the church on the Cliff. The present, third, church was built in 1734—51 according to a design by Antoni Müntzer and Antoni Solari

The crypt of the church on the Cliff was turned in 1880 into a national pantheon with graves of particularly outstanding scholars and artists

St. Catherine's Church endowed in 1363—26 by King Casimir the
Great. In the garden fragments of the old walls of the Kazimierz
district have survived

A picturesque corner in the area of the church on the Cliff: To the left,
the façade of St. Catherine's Church, in the centre, the tower of the
Church of Corpus Christi which forms part of the monastery of the
Canons Regular of the Lateran dating from 1340. The arch over the
street connects St. Catherine's Church with the Augustine convent

Kazimierz town hall in Wolnica Square, the main market place of the Kazimierz district, at present the Ethnographic Museum. In front of the building, *Three Players*, sculpted by Bronisław Chromy, 1964. Metal and stone

Old Synagogue (24 Szeroka Street), the oldest surviving Jewish sacral building in Poland, built in the 15th century, destroyed during the Second World War, subsequently reconstructed. At present, museum of the history of Cracow Jewry, a branch of the Historical Museum of the City of Cracow

The Wailing Wall in Poland's oldest Jewish cemetery, Rema (40 Szeroka Street), dating back to the 15th century. The wall is made of what remained of the old gravestones shattered by the Germans during the Second World War

which rests on one pillar, individual letters emblazoned on the keystones form together the name Kazymirus (Casimir), which is a confirmation that the church was founded by Casimir the Great.

Fate was not particularly kind to this church which suffered from fires and earthquakes and was devastated by the Austrians who turned it into a military storehouse. At present painstaking work is being carried out on its restoration and conservation. Beyond the convent towards the Vistula there stretch gardens enclosed to the north by a high wall, a remnant of the 14th century walls of Kazimierz.

Skałeczna Street ends with the **Cliff** (Skałka), once a rocky promontory (hence its name Skałka or rock). The Baroque **church** standing here and the buildings of the **Pauline monastery** (5) date back to 1734—51 and were built on the site of an earlier Romanesque rotunda and then a Gothic church. The latter is associated with the 11th century legend of Bishop Saint Stanislaus (Stanisław Szczepanowski), a story of strife between two strong powers: the secular power represented by King Boleslaus the Bold and the ecclesiastical power represented by the Bishop of Cracow. In 1079 the king condemned the bishop to death by beheading and as a result had to go into exile. The Church recognized the bishop as a martyr and years later canonized him. Legend has it that the sentence was carried out in the Church on the Cliff and though the bishop's remains rest in Wawel Cathedral this is the centre of his cult.

The vaults of the church contain a national pantheon which originated in the 19th century when on the 400th anniversary of the death of Jan Długosz his ashes were transferred to the Crypt of Honour in the church. Today the vaults hold the remains of the poets Wincenty Pol, Lucjan Siemieński, Teofil Lenartowicz and Adam Asnyk, the novelist Józef Ignacy Kraszewski, the playwright, poet and painter Stanisław Wyspiański, the painters Henryk Siemiradzki and Jacek Malczewski, the composer Karol Szymanowski, the actor Ludwik Solski and the astronomer Tadeusz Banachiewicz.

Krakowska Street leads farther on to WOLNICA SQUARE, Kazimierz's main market place and once a free market ("wolny"), hence its name. In the middle of the square stands a **town hall** (6) of the former town of Kazimierz, built in the 15th century, converted during the Renaissance, with its tower dating from the 16th century. In the 19th century the town hall was turned into a school building and since 1947 it has been the **Ethnographic Museum.**

In the north-eastern corner of the square you can see the **Corpus Christi Church** (7), built by King Casimir the Great, where King Ladislaus Jagiello brought the Bohemian Canons Regular of the Lateran. The showpieces of the interior of the church are: the Gothic stained-glass window dating from 1402 in the chancel, stalls carved in wood by the carpenter Stefan in 1624—32, a pulpit shaped like a boat, and the Renaissance epitaph slab of Bartolommeo Berrecci, the designer of the Sigismund Chapel, made by the artist himself who is buried in the local churchyard. During the siege of Cracow in 1655, King Charles Gustavus of Sweden had his headquarters in the Corpus Christi Church.

East of the Corpus Christi Church stretches the Jewish district. Its centre is SZEROKA STREET, along which three synagogues are situated: the Old, Rema and Poper synagogues. The **Old Synagogue** (8) at no. 24, built in the mid-15th century, was reconstructed in Renaissance style by Matteo Gucci following a fire in 1557. This is where Thaddeus Kosciuszko appealed to the Jewish community to join struggle for Poland's independence. During the Nazi occupation the building was partly ruined and the works of art that had been accumulated here over the centuries were looted. In the years 1955—57 the synagogue was restored and turned into a branch of the Historical Museum of the City of Cracow with a display entitled The History and Culture of Cracow Jewry.

The second synagogue, **Rema** (9), at no. 40, continues to serve its religious purpose. In 1553 Israel Isserles converted one of his houses into a house of prayer. The name of this smallest synagogue in Kazimierz is associated with the son of its founder, Rabbi Moses Isserles, the famous author and philosopher, who is buried in the cemetery by the syna-gogue. This cemetery, the origins of which go back to 1533, served the Jewish community until 1799. Before the Second World War there were still as many as 47 gravestones which were destroyed by the Germans. When after the war work began on the restoration of the Rema Synagogue, the conservators also became interested in the cemetery, where, right below the upper layer of earth, 700 gravestones were discovered, which apparently had been concealed from the Swedish army during their invasion of Poland. All of them were dug out, cleaned and placed in their original locations. Thanks to this we have now in Cracow Europe's only well-preserved Renaissance Jewish cemetery. Nearby, in Miodowa Street, there is another Jewish cemetery, 200 years old, with beautiful gravestones and avenues lined with old trees.

There are many more synagogues in Kazimierz: the **Poper Synagogue** (10) dating from 1620, which is now a Youth Club; the **Ajzyk Synagogue** (11) in 22 Jakuba Street, dating from 1638, with stucco decoration by Jan Falconi; the 16th century **High Synagogue** (12) at 38 Józefa Street, now occupied by the Historic Monuments Conservation Studios; the **Kupa Synagogue** (13) from 1590, at 8 Warszauera Street, the name of which indicates that it was built from kahal funds (*kupa* meaning purse); and the **Reformed Synagogue, the Tempel** (14), built in 1862, on the corner of Miodowa and Podbrzezie Streets, which still serves its original purpose.

The history of the Jewish population who had for centuries lived in Cracow ended during the Second World War. On 3 March 1941 the Nazis established a ghetto in the Cracow district of Podgórze which they encircled with a high wall which no one was allowed to approach on pain of being shot to death on the spot. Despite the terror, Poles helped the Jews enclosed in the ghetto. The history of this assistance is presented in the **Museum of National Remembrance in the Pharmacy under the Eagle,** at no. 18 Bohaterów Getta Square. The inhabitants of the ghetto were eventually deported by the Nazis to the death camps of Bełżec and Auschwitz and only a few survived.

CRACOW DISTRICTS

Administratively, Cracow is a city with voivodship status, divided into four main districts, the Centre, Nowa Huta, Podgórze and Krowodrza. Once there were more districts, the memory of which has survived in the names of streets or squares. Some of them once constituted separate towns (like Kazimierz or Kleparz), others formed suburban manors, settlements and villages which in time merged with the city.

ZWIERZYNIEC

The name of this district, meaning the bestiary, may have come either from a royal bestiary which could have been situated here, or else from the dense forests teeming with animals which here came up to the edge of the city. The most attractive part of Zwierzyniec is the **Błonia,** a meadow some 120 acres in area, which reaches almost to the city centre. The grazing of cows here is a time honoured tradition reverting to the privileges granted by the Polish kings to the local peasants. The Błonia is not just a meadow but also a place of popular fairs, mass rallies and sports events, for example the annual international parachuting competition.

Zwierzyniec, in the past a district inhabited by raftsmen, brick-layers and sand-diggers, has kept up many of the Cracow customs and traditions. By the Premonstratensian convent, the "Emaus" church fair each year attracts crowds of Cracovians on Easter Monday. From here eight days before Corpus Christi the Lajkonik procession starts for the Old Market Place. This is where most Cracow crèche makers, who display their Christmas cribs at the foot of the

Adam Mickiewicz statue in the Main Market Place in December, live.

The **church and convent of the Premonstratensian nuns** who arrived in 1162 from Bohemia, stands right by where the Rudawa flows into the Vistula which forms here a picturesque bend. Since the convent was situated far from the city, it was encircled by walls with towers which have been preserved. Nearby, on the slope of a hill, there are two more churches, Holy Saviour's and St. Margaret's.

Holy Saviour's is one of Cracow's oldest churches, built, according to legend, by Saint Adalbert who addressed the people from a stone pulpit still standing outside the church. The present building dates from 1662—73 and what has been left of the original 11th century edifice can be seen in a special trench dug under the floor.

On the opposite side of the street stands the wooden, octagonal **Church of St. Margaret,** dating from 1690. It is said that in pagan times this site was occupied by statues of the gods of wind, Świst and Poświst.

Proceeding up the street, the lower section of which is called, like the entire hill, after the BLESSED BRONI-SŁAWA (Bł. Bronisławy) and then turns into WASZYN-GTONA (Washington) Avenue, we pass to the left the **cemetery of the Saviour** where many outstanding Cracow authors, actors and painters are buried. The avenue goes as far as the old fortifications built by the Austrians during their occupation of Cracow. In 1977 these were turned into a **tourist hotel** called Pod Kopcem. On top of the hill of the Blessed Bronisława in 1820—23 Poles raised a **mound** in honour of the commander of the 1794 insurrection, **Thaddeus Kosciuszko.** The mound is 34.1 metres high and contains soil from the battlefields of Racławice, Maciejowice and Dubienka, and from America, all places where Kosciuszko fought. In 1862, the mound was topped with a boulder of Tatra granite, with the inscription *Kościuszce* (To Kosciuszko). On the western edge of the Wolski Forest, at Sowiniec, another **mound** was raised in 1936, in honour of **Marshal Józef Piłsudski.**

From Kosciuszko's Mound an attractive avenue leads to the **Wolski Forest** covering an area of a thousand acres, which is in fact a public park, with a zoological garden established in 1928 and, next to it, a café and a restaurant. On the edge of the forest on the side of Wola Justowska, there stands a small wooden church and a bit farther on an inn and a granary. Nearby stretches a **nature reserve** with old birch and oak trees and the Skały Panieńskie (Maidens' Cliffs) which legend associates with the Premonstratensian sisters who sought refuge here from the Tatars.

On Srebrna Góra (Silver Hill), in the part of the Wolski Forest by the Vistula, stands the **church and ermitage of the Camaldolese monks** who were brought to Poland in 1603. Inside, the church is sumptuously decorated with stucco work, sculptures and pictures, some of them painted by Tommaso Dolabella. In accordance with the rule of the monastery, only men are allowed inside the church. Women can enter it only on major holidays.

This part of the Wolski Forest is called Bielany where in the past Cracovians picnicked on Sundays in the shadow of oak trees. Today, on Whit Sunday, a grand fair is held here, with merry-go-rounds, shooting galleries and swings, and with stalls selling all those magnificent things that one can buy only during church fairs. The Cracow River Navigation company operates pleasure cruises in summer from Wawel to Bielany.

BRONOWICE

West of the city centre lies the district which only several dozen years ago was merely a village, Poland's most famous village, Bronowice, divided into two parts, Bronowice Duże and Bronowice Małe. Bronowice Duże was once a university estate which rector Hugo Kołłątaj parcelled out as part of his university reform. Bronowice Małe became famous due to the wedding of Jadwiga Mikołajczykówna, a local peasant girl, to the poet Lucjan Rydel. The wedding reception took place on 20 November 1900 and was depicted in Stanisław Wyspiański's celebrated drama, *The Wedding*, first produced on 16 March 1901 in the Municipal Theatre in Cracow. Literary critics say that in the period of the partitions, *The Wedding* was one of the major works which shaped national literature and theatre, that is, the Polish national consciousness.

The wedding house — a modest manor house called Rydlówka — has been turned, thanks to the family's generosity, into a **Regional Museum of the Polish Tourist Society** (PTTK). It is composed of a dancing room, where the band played, the guests danced and the ceremony of putting the cap on the bride's head was performed; the wedding room reconstructed exactly as Wyspiański described it; and a bed-chamber where family mementos, old photographs etc. are put on display.

Every year on the anniversary of the wedding, various festivities are held here, with performances of peasant rites and actors reciting excerpts of the drama.

ŁOBZÓW

One of the royal summer residences was situated north-west of Cracow, at a place called Łobzów, which today is part of the city. Once this was an area where royal hunts were held. In 1357 King Casimir the Great had a small hunting lodge built here which, gradually enlarged by Italian architects, including Santi Gucci and Giovanni Trevano, became a fairly large castle with what were perhaps the most beautiful gardens in Poland. This is where in 1595 King Ladislaus IV was born and this is where Queen Bona, King Henry of Valois and the papal legate Gaetano started their ceremonial processions before entering Cracow. In 1655 the Swedes completely plundered the castle which was restored by King John III (Sobieski) who set off on his expedition to Vienna from here. In 1777 King Stanislaus Augustus bequeathed the palace and the garden to Cracow University and in 1850 the Austrians turned it into a barracks, which it has remained until today.

View of the western suburbs of Cracow seen from the tower of St. Mary's Church with the Town Hall Tower in the foreground and the Kosciuszko Mound in the background

Not much has survived of the former splendour of the castle, while the gardens have disappeared without a trace.

KLEPARZ

A suburban settlement to the north of the centre of Cracow has existed from time immemorial and was mentioned for the first time as early as the 12th century.

The latest of the Cracow mounds, raised in 1936 in the Wolski Forest in honour of Marshal Józef Piłsudski

Zwierzyniec. Premonstratensian convent built in the 12th century far away from Cracow with strong fortifications. This is where the "Emaus", a traditional church fair, is held on Easter Monday and where the Lajkonik pageant begins eight days before Corpus Christi

Kosciuszko Mound (333 metres alt.) was raised in 1820—23 in honour of the commander of the national insurrection, Thaddeus Kosciuszko. Its summit commands a beautiful view of Cracow

Two major roads ran through it: one leading through the Florian Gate to Warsaw and the other from Silesia going under the Sławkowska Gate. Anyone who came late and found the city gates closed, spent the night in one of the numerous inns in Kleparz. In 1366 King Casimir the Great gave this place the name of Florencja (Florence) from the Church of St. Florian that existed here. This name however did not catch on and a new one appeared — Clepardia, the corruption of which, in the form of Kleparz, has survived until today. Kleparz had no town walls (only earthworks along part of its circumference) which is why

To the south-west of Cracow lies the Wolski Forest and closer to the Vistula, Bielany, together with its Camaldolese monastery at Silver Hill established in 1603 and built according to a design by the Italian architect Andrea Spezza. On Whit Sunday, church fairs are held at Bielany and in summer the place is reached by pleasure craft with jazz bands playing on board

each invasion meant total disaster for it. In 1792, it was incorporated into Cracow.

Today Kleparz boasts Cracow's largest market place. Its buildings date mostly from the late 19th and early 20th centuries, one notable exception being the **church and convent of the Visitation nuns** built in the late 17th century at no. 16 Krowoderska Street. Though situated outside the town walls, the convent has avoided fires and destruction and today you can admire here sumptuous Baroque interiors and an attractive façade regarded as one of the most beautiful in Cracow.

At Pędzichów beyond Kleparz the municipal gallows once stood.

WESOŁA

Historically this name, meaning joyful, is over 400 years old and today hardly anyone uses it. The central avenue of this eastern suburb of Cracow was the present Kopernika Street once lined by fine gardens, manor houses, country mansions and public gardens that attracted many inhabitants of the town.

The way to Wesoła from the city led under the Mikołajska (Nicholas) Gate, fragments of which are still to be seen when you look from the Planty park at the buildings of the Dominican convent. Next to it stood the Celestat, a shooting gallery of the Marksmen's Fraternity that has existed in Cracow for seven hundred years. Eight days before Corpus Christi, a new king of the marksmen is chosen.

Exactly opposite across the Planty there is the **Kazimierz Sosnowski Tourist Hostel (Dom Turysty)** that can accommodate 900 visitors. This is where Kopernika Street begins, which once lay along one of the oldest trade routes running from Cracow, via Mogiła, Wiślica, Sandomierz, Zawichost and farther on to Kiev where the cult of Saint Nicholas was widespread. Perhaps that is why the church standing just beyond the town walls is dedicated to Nicholas so that the arrivals from the east could be greeted by the saint they knew so well.

The **Church of St. Nicholas** stood here as early as 1105. Over the centuries it was reconstructed and converted repeatedly and its present interior is mostly in Baroque style. Worth special mention are the beautiful organ, played during frequently held concerts and, in front of the church, the lantern of the dead transferred from the St. Valentine's leprosarium in Kleparz, established in circa 1327. And this is probably how old this stone lantern is.

Today Kopernika Street has along its sides many clinics of the Medical Academy and several churches: the baroque **Church of St. Lazarus** at no. 19; the **Jesuit church** at no. 26, filled with modern works of art; and at no. 44, the **Carmelite church and convent** with a Gothic figure of the Madonna and Child dating from 1390. At the end of the street you will find the **Botanical Garden** laid out in 1783 by Hugo Kołłątaj and, at the entrance to the garden, the **Astronomical Observatory** built in 1788. Another, modern observatory is situated in Chełm, west of the Wolski Forest. Unfortunately, due to the pollution that makes the study of the sky impossible, this observatory too will have to move to a different location.

PODGÓRZE

This large industrial district of Cracow lies to the south, on the right bank of the Vistula. This area has always had many settlements and villages, and the local stone quarry in Krzemionki has supplied stone for the needs of the city. Following the first partition of Poland in 1772 the Vistula formed the border with Austria which planned to establish on its bank a city strong enough to rival or even to surpass Cracow. In 1784 the settlement of Podgórze was granted a municipal charter and numerous privileges meant to encourage new arrivals to settle in the free city, which status Podgórze obtained. These plans came to nought since in 1795 all Cracow fell prey to Austria. In the period of the

Duchy of Warsaw, in 1810, Podgórze was incorporated into Cracow; however, later, in 1815—46, when Cracow became a Free City, the Vistula again formed the border. Eventually Podgórze became part of Cracow in 1915.

Today Podgórze is above all an industrial district and its major manufacturers include a sodium plant, an electronics plant, a cable factory, a boiler fittings factory, a cosmetics factory and an artificial fertilizer plant.

On a hill that for centuries has been known as Krzemionki, rises the **Krakus Mound** (16 metres high), dating from the 6th—7th centuries, and next to it the small 11th century **Church of St. Benedict.** Here each year a church fair called Rękawka — since according to tradition in order to raise the mound the subjects of Prince Krakus carried earth in the sleeves of their cloaks (*rękaw* meaning sleeve in Polish) — is held on the Tuesday after Easter. Krzemionki is also the location of the Cracow TV centre and lower down, at the meeting point of the roads leading to Zakopane and Wieliczka, there is a spa, Mateczny, with excellent mineral waters.

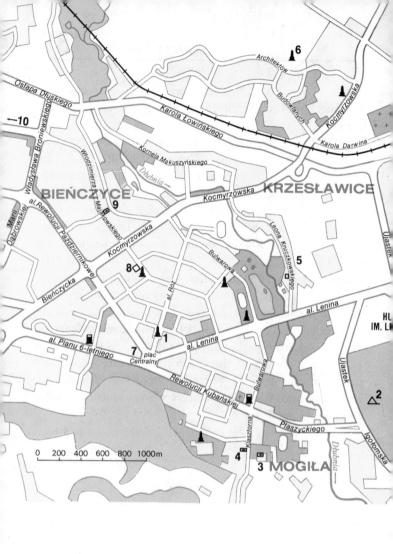

1. Lenin statue; 2. Mound of Wanda; 3. Cistercian abbey; 4. Church of St. Bartholomew; 5. Jan Matejko's manor house; 6. Memorial to the Victims of Nazism; 7. Community Centre; 8. Ludowy Theatre; 9. Church (Ark) of Our Lady Queen of Poland; 10. Church of St. Maximilian Kolbe

NOWA HUTA

The beginnings of this youngest and today the largest district of Cracow go back to 1949 when the decision to industrialize Poland was taken and a large metallurgical combine was built in the fields of the village of Mogiła east of the city together with a new town which today has over 220,000 inhabitants. It was named in 1954 after Lenin and at present produces half of Poland's iron and steel output.

The centre of this new town is CENTRALNY SQUARE from which the main streets radiate, lined with blocks of flats grouped in separate housing estates. On one of those main streets, Róż‹Avenue, stands the **Lenin Statue** (1), designed by Marian Konieczny and erected in 1971. As the town grew, new housing estates spilled onto the surrounding hills and the old airstrip of Czyżyny that separated Nowa Huta from Cracow's city centre.

While construction work was going on on the site of the steelworks, archaeologists were busy examining each foundation trench and their efforts yielded astonishing results. For they established that the villages that had to be liquidated to make room for the foundry (Mogiła, Pleszów, Bieńczyce and Krzesławice) were a continuation of old settlement and that some of them as early as two or three thousand years ago, had been industrial settlements where clay pots and bronze and iron products were manufactured. Magnificent ancient objects dating from that early period are today to be seen in the Nowa Huta branch of the Archaeological Museum and in the museum in Igołomia.

Nowa Huta is separated from the Lenin Metallurgical Combine by a hill topped by **Wanda's Mound** (2) which is 14 metres high and has on its summit a marble eagle on a pedestal, placed there in 1890. The age of the mound, as is also the case with the Mound of Krakus, has never been established. It is presumed that it was meant to serve as a guard post or signal post. The two mounds are Poland's highest prehistoric mounds. An old legend associated with Wanda's Mound says that Princess Wanda refused to marry the German commander of the invading army and conquered him in battle. However she decided to sacrifice herself to the gods and jumped into the waves of the Vistula, as a result of which the people raised a burial mound in her honour.

Nowa Huta also boasts a number of notable historic buildings. One of them is the **Cistercian abbey** (3) at Mogiła. The Cistercians settled here in the 13th century, built a magnificent church and a fortified monastery, and on the nearby river Dłubnia, a paper mill and fulleries, which used to export their products to Ruthenian dukedoms.

On the opposite side of KLASZTORNA STREET, in a clump of trees, stands the small wooden **Church of St. Bartholomew** (4) dating from the 14th century but repeatedly restored. Its oak wood Gothic portal still bears the date 1466.

The village of Mogiła is known from Wojciech Bogusławski's play *Krakowiacy i Górale* (Cracovians and Highlanders). On the site where the action of the play is presumed to take place you can see a commemorative stone placed there in 1971, with the inscription, "Wojciech Bogusławski, *Cracovians and Highlanders*, 1794 in the village of Mogiła."

In another part of Nowa Huta, Krzesławice on the Dłubnia, you can visit **Jan Matejko's manor house** (5), at 15 Kruczkowskiego Street, which at present belongs to the Society of the Friends of the Fine Arts. This house, boasting beautiful period furniture and surrounded by an old garden, is a museum dedicated to Jan Matejko as well as to Hugo Kołłątaj who once lived here. The Society of the Friends of the Fine Arts has in Nowa Huta, in Róż Avenue, its own exhibition rooms. Also in Krzesławice (near the tram-line terminal), stands a **monument mausoleum** (6) erected in 1957 in honour of 440 Polish patriots murdered in 1944 by the Nazis.

Among the relatively monotonous · buildings of Nowa Huta, some housing estates and facilities stand out by virtue of their attractive design. These include: the **Community Centre** (7) in Centralny Square, the **Ludowy Theatre** (8), at no. 34 Teatralne estate, and two churches, the **Ark of Our Lady Queen of Poland** (9) in Bieńczyce, shaped like a boat and lined outside with two million pebbles from mountain streams, and possessing an excellent organ (frequent concerts are held here), and the **Church of St. Maximilian Kolbe** (10), consecrated in 1983 by Pope John Paul II.

Despite the troublesome neighbourhood of the metallurgical combine, Nowa Huta has a lot of greenery, lawns adorned with sculptures, an artificial lake on the Dłubnia river and another one on the Vistula, with a **jetty** (10), and the Mogiła Forest, where Nowa Huta inhabitants take their walks and relax.

Lenin statue, in Róż Avenue, designed by Marian Konieczny, 1971

The Lenin Metallurgical Combine is Poland's largest steelworks, where furnace no. 1 produced pig iron for the first time on 22 July 1954

The construction of Nowa Huta began in 1949 and since then the town has developed dynamically amidst hills and greenery and at present is the home of 220,000 newcomers from all over Poland. Modernly laid out, it is a district of Cracow that is entirely different from the other parts of the city

Nowa Huta Bieńczyce. Modern church built in 1967—77, designed by Wojciech Pietrzyk and Jan Grabacki, consecrated in 1977 by Cardinal Karol Wojtyła

On 22 June 1983, during his second Polish pilgrimage, Pope John Paul II consecrated a church dedicated to St. Maximilian Kolbe in Nowa Huta. The church was built in 1976—83 according to a design by Józef Dutkiewicz

Ojców, an attractive holiday resort picturesquely situated in a deep valley in the Ojców National Park featuring magnificent ravines, gorges. limestone needles, gates in eroded rock, caves, rare species of animals and plants and also ruins — in the photo — of a 14th century castle

ENVIRONS

NIEPOŁOMICE
25 km east, by train or PKS bus

This small town lies at the edge of the Niepołomice Forest once teeming with wild animals and therefore frequently visited by Polish kings who held their hunts here and got their supplies of meat before military expeditions. In fact the forest is still a paradise for hunting, attracting Polish and foreign hunters with its wild boar and Carpathian stags. A special separate section of the forest is inhabited by bison, the most royal of the animals roaming in the Niepołomice Forest.

Niepołomice has a number of interesting sights. First, there is a **castle,** or a hunting lodge of the Polish kings. The first château was built here in the first half of the 14th century by King Casimir the Great. The present structure, a quadrangle with an arcaded courtyard, dates from the years 1550—71, and was designed by Tomasz Grzymała and decorated by Italian artists employed at Wawel castle. Although the capital of Poland was transferred to Warsaw, Niepołomice was still visited by Polish monarchs who came here for hunts. The last of them was the last king of Poland, Stanislaus Augustus, who arrived in Niepołomice in 1787 by special permission of Austria, since following the first partition of Poland it was incorporated into Austria.

While the castle was being built, King Casimir the Great also ordered, in 1350, the construction of a church which today contains interesting 14th century murals and a sarcophagus designed by Santi Gucci in the 16th century chapel of the Branicki family.

Kocmyrzów

Zastów

Proszowice

Dojazdów

ciborowice

KANTOROWICE

Tropiszów

ZESŁAWICE

ŁUCZANOWICE

GRĘBAŁÓW

WADÓW

Kocmyrzowska

JOWICE

LUBOCZA

KOŚCIELNIKI

Sandomierz

Dłubnia

KRZESŁAWICE

RUSZCZA

ENCZYCE

NOWA HUTA

Igołomska

NOWA
HUTA

HUTA IMIENIA LENINA

WYCIĄŻE

21

PLESZÓW

BRANICE

EG

MOGIŁA

20

Brzeska

LAS
MOGILSKI

KUJAWY

PRZYLASEK

Wisła

PRZEWÓZ

CHAŁUPKI

RYBITWY

NIEPOŁOMICE

Podłęże

CIM

BIEŻANÓW

Węgrzce Wielkie

Staniątki

4 Tarnów
E40 Przemyśl
Lwów

25 WIELICZKA

Szczakowa

Pieskowa
Skała

SKAŁA

SŁOMNIKI

JAWORZNO

Jerzmanowice

Ojców

Iwanowice

SIERSZA

Korzkiew

E77

Luborzyca

JELEŃ

A4

TRZEBINIA

Biały Kościół

4
E40

Michałowice

CHRZANÓW

KRZESZOWICE

Modlnica

Zielonki

Kocmyrzów

IN

Rudno

Zabierzów

Igołomia

LIBIĄŻ

A4

BALICE

NOWA HUTA

CHEŁMEK

Alwernia

Mników

BIELANY

KRAKÓW

Wisła

BOBREK

Babice

Liszki

NIEPOŁOMICE

OŚWIĘCIM

TYNIEC

4 E40

ZINKA

Spytkowice

SKAWINA

WIELICZKA

ZATOR

Brzeźnica

Wisła

Niegowić

Skawa

Mogilany

Świątniki
Górne

Gdów

Raba

KĘTY

WADOWICE

E462
96

KALWARIA
ZEBRZYDOWSKA

Głogoczów

DOBCZYCE

7
E77

niec

Gorzeń
Górny

Lanckorona

SUŁKOWICE

0   5   10   15kr

ANDRYCHÓW

Finally, you can see in Niepołomice a mound (14 metres high) raised in 1910—15 to commemorate the 500th anniversary of the battle of Grunwald.

WIELICZKA

15 km south-east, by PKS or city bus and train

Wieliczka borders on Cracow and soon it may become one of its districts. It is as old as Cracow. When in 1044 the Benedictines established an abbey in Tyniec, they derived part of their income from Wieliczka salt. Since salt was a product that was much sought after and the mines were raided by Tatars, King Casimir the Great had the town surrounded by walls with 11 towers and two gates, and built a royal castle. Wieliczka salt provided a third of all royal revenues and formed the basis of the fortunes accumulated by celebrated magnate families. In 1368 Casimir the Great issued the first miners' order, known as the Statute of the Cracow Salt Mines.

The thousand year old mine still operates today. Its oldest part was turned in 1950 into a museum which is a great tourist attraction. The length of the galleries and corridors amounts to some 200 kilometres of which some four kilometres are accessible to visitors. A tour of the mine and the museum lasts about three hours and takes in old pits, porches, underground lakes situated at 135 metres below ground level, chapels hewn from salt with altar-pieces and figures, a magnificent ball room, chambers

1. Old Town; 2. Wawel; 3. Błonia meadows; 4. Salwator; 5. Mound of Thaddeus Kosciuszko; 6. Mound of Marshal Józef Piłsudski; 7. Zoo; 8. Skały Panieńskie (Maidens' Cliffs) nature reserve; 9. Camaldolese church and monastery at Bielany; 10. Benedictine abbey at Tyniec; 11. "Rydlówka" regional museum of the Polish Tourist Society; 12. "Krak" motel and camping site; 13. Orbis motel and Holiday Inn hotel; 14. "Ogrodowy" camping site; 15. Rakowicki cemetery; 16. Lenin Museum; 17. Botanical Garden; 18. Museum of Aviation and Aeronautics; 19. Academy of Physical Training; 20. Cistercian abbey at Mogiła; 21. Mound of Wanda; 22. Mound of Krakus; 23. Mateczny; 24. "Krakowianka" camping site and hotel; 25. Salt mine at Wieliczka; 26. Forum hotel

completely lined in wood, original machinery that is hundreds of years old and even an underground tennis court. There is also an underground sanatorium, Kinga, where chronic allergic diseases are treated.

The name of the sanatorium derives from a legend about Princess Kinga, the daughter of King Béla IV of Hungary, who in 1239 married Prince Boleslaus the Bashful of Cracow. Hungary had large deposits of salt and Kinga wanted her new homeland to possess similar riches. Therefore on leaving Hungary she dropped her ring into the mine pit and when she arrived in Poland she ordered digging at Wieliczka where in a lump of salt her ring was found.

In the 17th century the French traveller Jean Le Laboureur compared the Wieliczka mines with the pyramids and said that they are "no less magnificent than the Egyptian pyramids but more useful. They are a glorious memento of the Poles' industriousness."

WADOWICE
55 km south-west, by train or PKS bus

This small town boasts rich cultural traditions. As early as 1327 it obtained a town charter and was an important point on the trade route between Cracow and Silesia. In 1494 it was purchased by King John Albert and together with the dukedom of Zator became part of the Crown territories. Many crafts developed here and in the 19th century, the foodstuffs, building materials and paper industries. Wadowice is also an important railway and road junction.

Wadowice was the birthplace of Marcin Wadowita (b. 1567), for many years rector of Cracow University and an outstanding scholar; of the poet and novelist Emil Zegadłowicz (1888—1941), who was one of the founders of the Czartak poetic group and lived in a manor house in Gorzeń Górny near Wadowice; and of Karol Wojtyła, the present Pope John Paul II, born on 18 May 1920 in a house in the narrow Kościelna Street.

Wieliczka salt mine. Chapel of the Blessed Kinga. Bas-relief representation of the *Flight into Egypt* carved in salt by Andrzej Wyrodek

Wieliczka salt mine. Lake in the Weimar chamber with a beautifully restored wooden ceiling and a figure of St. John of Nepomuk

Wieliczka salt mine. General view of the underground chapel of the Blessed Kinga dating from the late 19th and early 20th centuries, sculpted by the brothers Józef and Tomasz Markowski and Andrzej Wyrodek

Wieliczka salt mine, 18the century "Hungarian" treadmill in the Kraj chamber that used to be operated by four pairs of horses. The first horse-driven treadmills appeared in Wieliczka in the early 17th century

Wieliczka salt mine. Underground allergological sanatorium established in 1964, situated at the depth of 200 metres

Wadowice, 7 Kościelna Street. The family home of the present pope. The plaque in the wall says: "Here on 18 May 1920 Karol Józef Wojtyła, Pope John Paul II, was born and lived thereafter"

Wadowice. The room where Pope John Paul II was born. His parents, Karol and Emilia née Kaczorowska, occupied a small two-room flat on the first floor

Not many period houses have survived in Wadowice. Apart from several burgher houses in the centre, there are the parish church dating from the 15th—16th centuries in the market place, and the classicist **Mikołaj manor house,** built in the early 19th century by the administrator of Wadowice, Mikołaj Komorowski.

In 1939 in the area of Wadowice, the "Kraków" Army fought a battle with the German troops and during the occupation Wadowice was an important contact point for the underground Home Army in communications between the General Government and Cieszyn Silesia, Transolsania and Slovakia.

TYNIEC
12 km west, by city bus

High above the Vistula, on a steep white cliff, stands a fortified monastery and church. This is the Benedictine abbey founded in the 11th century by Casimir the Restorer. The river flows here through a narrow valley, forming a gorge in the rocks of the Cracow Upland, and a fortified structure at this point sealed access to Cracow. Archaeologists have established that as early as the 8th—5th century B.C. this site was occupied by a fortified settlement of the peoples of the Lusatian culture.

The Tyniec fortress had its own garrison. From here the confederates of Bar, on the night of 1 to 2 February 1772, set off on the notorious raid against Cracow during which they seized Wawel. Unfortunately, in the same year Tyniec was captured by the Russian army and completely destroyed. In 1817, as a result of the abolition of the Benedictine order, the monks had to leave the monastery. Following a fire in 1821, the fortress, church and monastery fell into complete ruin. In 1939 the hill of Tyniec again became the property of the Benedictines and in 1969 Tyniec recovered the title of abbey. For several dozen years the reconstruction of the whole complex has been going on and the monastery is slowly regaining its former splendour.

To reach the courtyard you must pass under two fortified gates. Part of the courtyard is occupied by the church with two great towers and next to it the monastery. In the centre you can see a well, hewn from the rock in 1620, with a windlass and an octagonal roof constructed without the use of a single nail. In summer, between May and September, organ recitals attracting many music lovers are held in the church.

OŚWIĘCIM (AUSCHWITZ)
50 km west by PKS bus or train

This town became notorious all over the world. In 1940 the Nazis established here, just outside the town, their largest **concentration camp, Auschwitz-Birkenau.** The Polish inhabitants were evicted from the surrounding area and a death zone many kilometres wide was laid out round the camp to prevent the local population from learning about the crimes committed and escaped prisoners from getting help. According to the findings of the Nuremberg tribunal, throughout the existence of the camp the Nazis murdered there some four million people. Whole trainloads of people were sent to the gas chambers of Birkenau, capable of exterminating 60,000 within 24 hours with the help of Cyclon B gas produced by I.G. Farben. The bodies of the victims were burnt in crematoria and on open pyres and the ashes were scattered in nearby marshes. People from all over Europe perished here: Poles, Jews, Gypsies, Russians, Frenchmen, Yugoslavs, Dutch, Belgians, Germans and others. This is the largest and most cruel cemetery in the world.

On the site of the Auschwitz camp there is a museum which apart from permanent exhibitions dedicated to the memory of the victims and documenting the Nazi crimes, has an archive and conducts large-scale research. The site of the camp in Birkenau has been left in the state it was in when the Germans abandoned it. At the end of the railway siding where transports of prisoners arrived, there stands a

Tyniec. Fortified Benedictine abbey established in the 11the century. Today Tyniec is famous for its ancient architecture and magnificent concerts of organ music

Monument to the Martyrdom of Nations unveiled in 1967 commemorates the death of four million victims murdered by the Germans during the Second World War in the concentration camp of Auschwitz-Birkenau. The monument was designed by Pietro Cascella, Jerzy Jarnuszkiewicz, Julian Pałka and Giorgio Simoncini

Ruins of the Birkenau crematoria blown up by the Germans fleeing before the Red Army in January 1945

The Death Wall in Auschwitz where executions were held

Pieskowa Skała castle situated within the Ojców National Park. The first castle on this site was built in the 11th century. The present Renaissance structure dates from the 16th century. Once it was a hideout of knightly robbers. At present, a branch of the Wawel State Art Collections

monument to the memory of all those murdered. The monument was designed by Polish and Italian artists.

OJCÓW
25 km north-west, by PKS bus

Not far from the centre of Cracow there lies a picturesque deep valley which, almost in its entirety, forms the **Ojców National Park.** This is in fact a canyon in steep white limestone rock cut across by the river Prudnik. This is where one of Poland's most attractive tourist routes begins, the Route of the Eagles' Nests, with old châteaux, most of them now in ruin, that used to guard the ancient trade route connecting Cracow with Silesia. In the closest vicinity, you may visit the ruins of the châteaux in Korzkwia and Ojców and the excellently preserved castle in Pieskowa Skała.

The Ojców Valley is the longest (15 km) and most picturesque of the valleys in the entire Cracow-Wieluń Upland. The Ojców National Park is not large (less than 4,000 acres) but extremely attractive, with beautiful gorges, valleys, rocky needles, gates and maces, and with 50 caves, the largest of which are Zbójecka (170 metres long), Łokietka (250 metres) and Ciemna (150 metres). The Ojców Valley is the habitat of over 2,600 animal species, including 1,600 butterfly species, and the *gniewosz*, Poland's only tree snake, which kills its prey, mostly mice, by strangulation. This is also the only place where you can see the Ojców birch *(betula Oycoviensis).*

The restored Gothic **tower** in the ruins of the Ojców castle holds a display of Ojców flora and fauna and an archaeological exhibition. Several kilometres away, in **Pieskowa Skała,** you may visit a castle, formerly a hideout of knightly robbers and today a well-preserved example of Renaissance defensive architecture, which houses a branch of the Wawel State Art Collections, with an exhibition demonstrating changes in style in European art from the Middle Ages to the 19th century. The southern bastion of the wall is a popular tourist restaurant.

The rock at the foot of the castle bears a commemorative tablet and a mausoleum with the ashes of the Russian captain Andrei Potebnya and 63 Polish insurgents of 1863 who all were killed in the struggle against the tsarist army for the freedom of Poland.

Nearby, you should see a lone rock, called Sokolica or Hercules' Mace, which was climbed for the first time as late as 1932.

PRACTICAL INFORMATION

"IT" Tourist Information Centre, ul. Pawia 8, tel. 22-04-71 and 22-60-91

Almatur Travel Office of the Polish Students' Association, Rynek Główny 7/8, tel. 22-67-08, telex 032 5214

"BORT" Polish Tourist and Sightseeing Society, ul. Solskiego 26, tel. 22-83-05

"GROMADA" Tourist Cooperative, pl. Szczepański 6, tel. 22-49-39 and 22-37-45, telex 032 2432

"Harc-Tour" Tourist Office of the Polish Pathfinders' Union, ul. Karmelicka 31, tel. 33-93-29, telex 032 2583

Juventur Voivodship Tourist Office of the Polish Socialist Youth Union, ul. Sławkowska 3, tel. 22-24-37 and 22-10-86, telex 032 2530

Logos-Tour Travel Office of the Polish Teachers' Union, ul. Czysta 1, tel. 34-03-25, telex 032 2615

Polish Baltic Shipping, ul. Pawia 6, tel. 22-71-14, telex 032 5355

"Orbis" Travel Bureau, Incoming Tourist Office, al. Puszkina 1, tel. 22-28-85, telex 032 2403, ul. Koniewa 7, tel. 37-05-10, telex 032 5324

Polish Motoring Association, Regional Tourist Office, ul. Sarego 5, tel. 22-34-90 and 22-51-77, telex 032 2310

"Sports-Tourist" Sports and Tourist Office, ul. św. Jana 18, tel. 22-95-10 and 22-47-30, telex 032 2237

"Turysta" Cooperative Tourist Office, pl. Szczepański 6, tel. 22-81-64 and 22-97-24, telex 032 5404

"Wawel-Tourist" Cracow Tourist Office, Incoming Bureau, ul. Pawia 6/8, tel. 22-41-62 and 22-08-81, telex 032 2516

HOTELS

"Orbis" Hotels

Cracovia****, al. Puszkina 1, tel. 22-86-66 (switchboard) and 22-13-43 (reception desk), telex 032 2341

Forum****, ul. Konopnickiej 28, tel. 66-95-00, telex 032 2737

Holiday Inn****, ul. Koniewa 7, tel. 37-50-44 (switchboard) and 37-00-75 (reception desk), telex 032 5356

Motel Orbis****, ul. Koniewa 9, tel. 37-16-77, telex 032 5507

Francuski***, ul. Pijarska 13, tel. 22-51-22 and 22-52-70, telex 032 2253

Other Hotels

"Wawel-Tourist" Hotel Reservation, ul. Pawia 6, tel. 22-15-09 (advance bookings), telex 032 5355, open 9 a.m. to 3 p.m., on weekdays and the last Saturday of each month; tel. 22-97-30 (current bookings)

Europejski**, ul. Lubicz 5, tel. 22-09-11, 22-89-25 and 22-84-55

Monopol***, ul. Waryńskiego 6, tel. 22-76-26 and 22-76-66, telex 032 5710

Polonia**, ul. Basztowa 25, tel. 22-16-61 and 22-12-81

Polski***, ul. Pijarska 17, tel. 22-11-44, 22-14-26, 22-13-27 and 22-15-29, telex 032 5712

Pod Kopcem***, al. Waszyngtona, tel. 22-03-55 (switchboard) and 22-20-55 (reception desk), telex 032 2609

Pod Różą***, ul. Floriańska 14, tel. 22-93-99, 22-47-83, 22-12-44 and 22-14-24, telex 032 5340

Saski**, ul. Sławkowska 3, tel. 21-42-22, telex 032 5779

Pod Złotą Kotwicą**, ul. Szpitalna 20, tel. 22-10-44 and 22-11-28

Warszawski*, ul. Pawia 6, tel. 22-06-22 and 22-97-30

Krak****, ul. Radzikowskiego 99, tel. 37-21-22, 37-53-40, 37-27-94 and 37-23-72, telex 032 5698

Almatur International Student Hotel (open 1 July to 15 Sept.), al. 29 Listopada 48a; reception desk in Merkury Student Hostel, tel. 11-44-55. Take bus 105 from the square by the Central Railway Station

CAMPING SITES

Krak**** (no. 45 of the Polish Camping Federation), "Wawel-Tourist", ul. Radzikowskiego 99, tel. 37-21-22, telex 032 5698. Camping field for about 600 tourists and stands for about 85 caravans

Krakowianka*** (no. 171 of the PCF), "Krakowianka" Sports and Recreation Centre, Borek Fałęcki, ul. Żywiecka Boczna, tel. 66-41-91 and 66-41-92. With a camping field and caravan stands

Kemping Ogrodowy*** (no. 103 of the PCF), ul. Królowej Jadwigi 223, tel. 22-20-11 ext. 67. Accommodation for 100 tourists

Wieliczka: Kinga**** (PCF no. 238), "Wawel-Tourist", ul. Kościuszki 36, tel. 78-27-00. Camping field for 100 tourists and caravan facilities

IMPORTANT ADDRESSES AND TELEPHONE NUMBERS

Address Register, pl. Wiosny Ludów 3/4, tel. 22-24-44 ext. 225, open 8 a.m. to 3.30 p.m., on Mondays 9 a.m. to 5 p.m. and on Saturdays 8 a.m. to 12 noon

Railway Inquiries, Central Railway Station; domestic timetable tel. 933, international timetable tel. 22-41-82 and 22-22-48

Long Distance Bus (PKS) Inquiries, Bus Station, pl. Kolejowy 1, tel. 936, 7 a.m. to 3 p.m.

LOT Airlines Inquiries, ul. Basztowa 15, tel. 22-50-76 and 22-70-78, telex 032 2254, open on weekdays 8 a.m. to 6 p.m.

Airport Balice, tel. 11-67-00, telex 032 2411

Emergency telephones
Ambulance service tel. 999
Fire brigade tel. 998
Police (MO) tel. 997

Long-distance dialing codes

Biała Podlaska 0-801*
Biały Dunajec 0-165
Bochnia 0-197
Brzesko 0-192
Bukowina Tatrzańska 0-1657111
Chochołów 0-187
Czarny Dunajec 0-187
Czorsztyn 0-18777
Gdańsk 0-58
Gdynia 0-58
Gniezno 0-661
Gorzów Wielkopolski 0-95
Jabłonka Orawska 0-621
Kalisz 0-187
Katowice 0-32
Krynica 0-135
Leszno 0-651
Łódź 0-42
Lublin 0-81
Muszyna 0-1351511
Myślenice 0-115

Niedzica 0-18777
Nowy Sącz 0-181
Nowy Targ 0-187
Ostrów Wielkopolski 0-641
Piwnicza 0-18133511
Piła 0-671
Płock 0-24
Poronin 0-165
Poznań 0-61
Siedlce 0-251
Sopot 0-58
Środa Wielkopolska 0-665
Sromowce Wyżne 0-18777
Stary Sącz 0-181
Tarnów 0-141
Warsaw 0-22
Wrocław 0-71
Września 0-665
Zakopane 0-165
Zielona Góra 0-68

International dialing codes

Bulgaria 0-035
Czechoslovakia 0-042
Finland 0-040
France 0-033
Germany, Federal Republic of 0-049
Great Britain 0-044

Netherlands 0-031
Spain 0-034
Switzerland 0-041

Telephone exchange for other out-of town calls 900
Long-distance calls operator 909
Local inquiries 911
Telegrammes 905
Early morning calls 917
Local information 913

---

* After dialing "0" an uninterrupted dial tone must be heard; only then should the actual telephone number be dialed.

GUIDE SERVICES

Guides speaking Polish and foreign languages for sightseeing tours of Cracow and its vicinity can be hired from BORT PTTK, ul. Szpitalna 32, tel. 22-41-44 (group and individual tours)

ROAD SERVICE

"Polmozbyt" Emergency Service, Cracow, al. Pokoju 81, tel. 48-00-84, weekdays 6 a.m. to 10 p.m., Saturdays and Sundays 10 a.m. to 6 p.m.

PZMot, Nowa Huta, al. Planu 6-letniego 154, tel. 44-17-60 and 44-16-32, weekdays 7 a.m. to 10 p.m., Saturdays, Sundays and holidays 10 a.m. to 6 p.m.

Bidziński, Janusz, Cracow, ul. Karłowicza 9/8, tel. 33-91-48

Dawidowicz, Ryszard, Cracow, ul. Koniewa 55/24, tel. 37-08-20

Dobrzyński, Andrzej, Cracow, ul. Tarłowska 4/2, tel. 22-05-57

Durmała, Stanisław, Słomniki, ul. Kościuszki 55

Horak, Krzysztof, Cracow, ul. Mikołajska 3/6

Jankowski, Henryk, os. Kazimierzowskie 18/319

Kafin, Piotr, os. Krzesławice, ul. Wąwozowa 30

CAR PARKS WITH ATTENDANT (open round the clock)

pl. św. Ducha (only cars)
pl. Biskupi (only cars)
pl. Szczepański (only cars)
ul. Włóczków (cars and lorries)
Cracovia hotel (cars and minibuses)
ul. Powiśle (cars and coaches)
ul. Kałuży (cars and coaches)
ul. Kopernika next to the Dom Turysty (cars and coaches)
ul. Koniewa by Holiday Inn (no restrictions)
ul. 18 Stycznia by the Pewex shop (cars only)
ul. Teligi — Wielicka (no restrictions)
ul. Bohaterów Stalingradu (cars only)

PETROL STATIONS

ul. Gagarina, tel. 37-04-70, open round the clock
ul. Kamienna, tel. 11-96-38, open round the clock
ul. Nowopłaszowska, open round the clock
ul. Koniewa, tel. 37-45-27, open weekdays 6 a.m. to 10 p. m., Sundays and holidays 7 a.m. to 10 p.m.
ul. Mogilska 116, tel. 11-41-75, open weekdays 6 a.m. to 10 p.m., Sundays and holidays 7 a.m. to 10 p.m.

ul. Pilotów, tel. 11-63-15, open weekdays 6 a.m. to 10 p.m. Sundays and holidays 7 a.m. to 8 p.m.

ul. Radzikowskiego 4, tel. 37-40-94, open weekdays 6 a.m. to 10 p.m., Sundays and holidays 7 a.m. to 6 p.m.

ul. 18 Stycznia, open weekdays 6 a.m. to 10 p.m., Sundays and holidays 7 a.m. to 10 p.m.

u. Wielicka 119, tel. 55-04-24, open weekdays 6 a.m. to 10 p.m., Saturdays 6 a.m. to 6 p.m.

ul. Wioślarska, open weekdays 6 a.m. to 10 p.m, Sundays and holidays 7 a.m. to 10 p.m.

ul. Bulwarowa, Nowa Huta, open weekdays 6 a.m. to 10 p.m., Sundays and holidays 7 a.m. to 10 p.m.

Czyżyny, Nowa Huta, open weekdays 6 a.m. to 10 p.m., Sundays and holidays 7 a.m. to 8 p.m.

os. Strusia, Nowa Huta, tel. 48-51-85, open round the clock

ul. Włóczków, tel. 22-77-63, open weekdays 6 a.m. to 10 p.m., Sundays and holidays 7 a.m. to 10 p.m.

and by major communications arteries

CALOR-GAS RE-FILLING

ul. Radzikowskiego 180, tel. 37-40-61, open daily with the exception of Saturdays 7 a.m. to 2 p.m. (re-filling, repair and checking)

ul. Wioślarska (petrol station), open weekdays 6 a.m. to 10 p.m., Sundays 7 a.m. to 10 p.m.

ul. Powstańców Wielkopolskich (petrol station), Wednesdays and Saturdays 10 a.m. to 4 p.m.

FOREIGN CONSULATES

France, ul. Stolarska 15, tel. 22-33-90 (secretariat) and 22-21-13. Visa section open daily with the exception of Saturdays, Sundays and holidays, 9 a.m. to 12 noon

USSR, ul. Westerplatte 11, tel. 22-26-47 and 22-83-88, open Mondays, Wednesdays and Fridays 8.30 a.m. to 12.30 p.m.

United States, ul. Stolarska 9, tel. 22-14-00 (visas and passports 8.30 a.m. to 12 noon), 22-77-93 and 22-97-64, open daily with the exception of Saturdays, Sundays and holidays, 8.30 a.m. to 5 p.m.

MUSEUMS

State Art Collections of Wawel, Wawel 5, tel. 22-51-55 and 22-57-47
Royal Chambers, open Tuesdays, Thursdays, Saturdays and Sundays 10 a.m. to 3 p.m., Wednesdays and Fridays 12 noon to 6 p.m. (closed on Mondays and days following holidays)

Crown Treasury and Armoury, open daily with the exception of Mondays 10 a.m. to 3.15 p.m.

Exhibition "Wawel That Is no More", open daily with the exception of Tuesdays 10 a.m. to 3.30 p.m.

The East in the Wawel Collections, visiting by previous appointment with the Educational Division, tel. 22-51-55 ext. 180

Royal Tombs and Sigismund Bell, open daily 9 a.m. to 3 p.m., on Sundays 12.15 to 3 p.m.

Cathedral Museum, open daily with the exception of Mondays 10 a.m. to 3 p.m.

Dragon's Cave at the foot of Wawel Hill near the Thief's Tower open between 1 June and 30 Sept., daily with the exception of Mondays 10 a.m. to 3 p.m.

National Museum, Central Administration, ul. Manifestu Lipcowego 12, tel. 22-27-33 and 22-27-63

Branches:

Jan Matejko's House, ul. Floriańska 41, tel. 22-59-26 (Jan Matejko's paintings, drawings, artistic collections and souvenirs). Open Wednesdays, Thursdays, Saturdays and Sundays 10 a.m. to 4 p.m., Fridays 12 noon to 6 p.m.

Painting Gallery in the Cloth Hall, Rynek Główny, tel. 22-11-66 (Polish painting and sculpture from 1764 to 1900). Open Mondays, Fridays, Saturdays and Sundays 10 a.m. to 4 p.m., Thursdays 12 noon to 6 p.m.

Szołayski House, pl. Szczepański 9, tel. 22-70-21 (Polish painting and sculpture up to 1765). Open Mondays, Wednesdays, Saturdays and Sundays 10 a.m. to 4 p.m., Tuesdays 12 noon to 6 p.m.

Stanisław Wyspiański Museum, ul. Kanonicza 9, tel. 22-83-37 (Stanisław Wyspiański's paintings, publications and souvenirs). Open Wednesdays, Fridays, Saturdays and Sundays 10 a.m. to 4 p.m., Thursdays 12 noon to 6 p.m.

New Building, al. 3 Maja 1, tel. 34-33-77 (Polish painting and sculpture from the late 19th cent. until the present day). Open Thursdays, Fridays, Saturdays and Sundays 10 a.m. to 3.30 p.m., Wednesdays 12 noon to 5.30 p.m.

Tapestry Section, ul. Smoleńsk 9, tel. 22-15-31

Czartoryski Collection, ul. św. Jana 19, tel. 22-55-66 (historical mementos and European painting). Open Mondays, Tuesdays, Saturdays and Sundays 10 a.m. to 4 p.m., Fridays 12 noon to 6 p.m.

No admission charge on the days when the museums are open from 12 noon.

Historical Museum of the City of Cracow, Central Administration, Rynek Główny 35, tel. 22-99-22 and 22-65-27

Branches:

Krzysztofory, Rynek Główny 35, tel. 22-99-22 (Cracow's history and culture). Open Wednesdays, Fridays, Saturdays and Sundays 9 a.m. to

3 p.m., Thursdays 11 a.m. to 6 p.m. Closed on second Saturday and Sunday of each month in which case open additionally on Monday and Tuesday

Military Collections and Clocks, ul. św. Jana 12, tel. 22-53-98. Open Thursdays, Fridays, Saturdays and Sundays 9 a.m. to 3 p.m., Wednesdays 11 a.m. to 6 p.m. Closed on first Saturday and Sunday of each month

History of the Cracow Theatre, ul. Szpitalna 21, tel. 22-68-64

Robert Jahoda's Printing and Book-binding Press, ul. Gołębia 4, tel. 22-99-22 (history of Cracow printing and book-binding). Open daily 10 a.m. to 2 p.m. Closed on first Saturday and Sunday of each month

Town Hall Tower, Rynek Główny (insignia of office of town mayors, state decorations, weapons carried by municipal guard). Open Wednesdays, Fridays, Saturdays and Sundays 9 a.m. to 3 p.m., Thursdays 11 a.m. to 6 p.m. Closed on second Saturday and Sunday of each month

Poles' Struggle and Martyrdom in 1939—45, ul. Pomorska 2, tel. 33-41-00. Open Wednesdays, Fridays, Saturdays and Sundays 9 a.m. to 3 p.m., Thursdays 11 a.m. to 6 p.m. Closed on second Saturday and Sunday of each month in which case open additionally on Monday and Tuesday

Museum of the History and Culture of Cracow Jewry, Old Synagogue, ul. Szeroka 24, tel. 66-05-44. Open Wednesdays, Thursdays, Saturdays and Sundays 9 a.m. to 3 p.m., Fridays 11 a.m. to 6 p.m. Closed on first Saturday and Sunday of each month in which case open additionally on Monday and Tuesday 9 a.m. to 3 p.m.

Museum of National Remembrance, Pharmacy "Under the Eagle", pl. Bohaterów Getta 18. During the Nazi occupation this chemist's shop situated in the area of the former ghetto was a transit point for relief supplies provided by Poles to Jews. Open daily with the exception of Mondays

Archaeological Museum, ul. Poselska 3, tel. 22-75-60 and 22-77-61 (ancient and mediaeval history of the Little Poland region, ancient history of Nowa Huta, Egyptian mummies displayed under x-rays). Open Mondays 9 a.m. to 2 p.m., Tuesdays, Thursdays and working Saturdays 2 to 6 p.m., Fridays 10 a.m. to 2 p.m., and Sundays 11 a.m. to 2 p.m. Free admission on Thursdays

Cellars of St. Adalbert's Church, Rynek Główny (history of the Main Market Place). Open Mondays, Tuesdays, Thursdays, Fridays and Saturdays 9 a.m. to 4 p.m., Wednesdays 9 a.m. to 1 p.m., and Sundays 1 to 5 p.m.

Ethnographic Museum, pl. Wolnica 1, tel. 66-28-63 (Polish folk culture). Open Wednesdays, Thursdays, Fridays, Saturdays and Sundays 10 a.m. to 3 p.m., and Mondays (free admission) 10 a.m. to 6 p.m.

Museum of Aviation and Aeronautics, al. Planu 6-letniego 17, tel. 44-71-81 (aircraft, helicopters, aircraft engines, experimental rockets). Open between 1 May and 31 Oct., daily with the exception of Mondays 10 a.m. to 2 p.m.

Lenin's Museum, ul. Topolowa 5, tel. 21-03-79. Open Tuesdays and Fridays 9 a.m. to 6 p.m., Wednesdays 9 a.m. to 5 p.m., Saturdays 10 a.m. to 5 p.m., Sundays 10 a.m. to 3 p.m. and Thursdays 9 a.m. to 4 p.m. Admission free

Lenin's Home, ul. Królowej Jadwigi 41, tel. 22-59-38. Open daily with the exception of Thursdays 9 a.m. to 3 p.m. Admission free

Regional Museum of Young Poland "Rydlówka", PTTK, Bronowice Małe, ul. Włodzimierza Tetmajera 28, tel. 37-07-50 (folk art and customs in the vicinity of Cracow, special display devoted to the participants in the wedding reception of the poet Rydel). Open Tuesdays, Wednesdays, Fridays, and Saturdays 11 a.m. to 3 p.m., Thursdays 3 to 7 p.m. Closed on Mondays, Sundays and holidays

Museum of the Jagiellonian University, ul. Jagiellońska 15, tel. 22-05-49 (Collegium Maius: History of the University). Open daily with the exception of Sundays and holidays 12 noon to 2 p.m. (group tours by previous appointment by telephone)

Natural History Museum of the Polish Academy of Sciences, ul. Sławkowska 17, tel. 22-59-59 (Polish fauna). Open daily with the exception of Mondays 10 a.m. to 1 p.m. Admission free

Museum of Pharmacology of the Medical Academy, ul. Basztowa 3, tel. 22-38-53 (18th cent. chemist's shop, laboratory dating from the late 16th and early 17th cent., history of chemist's vessels, collection of medicinal raw materials and preparations, weighs and scales). Open by previous appointment by telephone daily 10 a.m. to 12 noon, with the exception of Saturdays, Sundays and holidays

Museum of the History of Photography named after Professor Władisław Bogacki. Rynek Główny 17 (collection of photographic equipment, mementos of photographers, old photographs, unique autochromes dating from 1902—13, reading room and library).

Ojców National Park: Władysław Szafer Museum, "Łokietek" villa, Ojców, tel. 40 (geology and geomorphology of the Prądnik valley, traces of old cultures in the vicinity of Ojców). Open between 1 May and 31 Oct., daily with the exception of Mondays, 9 a.m. to 4 p.m. During the rest of the year, visits by previous appointment with the administration of the Ojców National Park

Ojców: Museum of the Polish Tourist Society (PTTK), Castle Tower (archaeological and ethnographic collection from the area). Open only by previous appointment between 15 April and 31 Oct. daily 10 a.m. to 5 p.m., with the exception of Mondays

Ojców: Ladislaus the Short's Cave. Open between 1 May and 31 Oct. daily 8 a.m. to 7 p.m. During the rest of the year visits by previous appointment with BORT PTTK in Ojców

Pieskowa Skała Museum (branch of the Wawel State Art Collections), tel. Sułoszowa 4 or Olkusz 11 (changes in European art from the Middle Ages to the mid-19th cent.). Open Wednesdays, Thursdays, Fridays, Saturdays and Sundays 10 a.m. to 3.30 p.m., Tuesdays 12 noon to 5.30 p.m. Closed on Mondays and days following holidays

Wieliczka Salt Mine, ul. Daniłowicza 10, tel. Cracow 78-10-40, 78-10-71, 78-12-33, 22-15-50 and 22-03-92 ext. 302. Open between 15 April and 31 Oct. daily 8 a.m. to 5 p.m. (last visitors admitted 5 p.m.) and between 2 Nov. and 14 April 8 a.m. to 3 p.m. (last visitors admitted at 3 p.m.). The tourist route covers twenty old chambers connected by corridors 2,613 metres in length (about two hours)

Wieliczka: Museum of Cracow Salt Mines, Park bł. Kingi, tel. Cracow 78-32-66 and 22-19-47. Closed on Mondays. The Museum encompasses 15 chambers with displays, connected by corridors 1,436 metres in length, about one hour. Ancient salt mining and salt works, geology of salt deposits, history of the Cracow Salt Mines and the mining towns of Wieliczka and Bochnia, archaeology of the region.

State Museum of Auschwitz-Birkenau — Museum of Martyrdom of the Polish Nation, Oświęcim, ul. Więźniów Oświęcimia 20, tel. 240-21 and 220-21. Open between 1 June and 31 Aug. 8 a.m. to 7 p.m. and between 1 Sept. and 30 May 8 a.m. to 6 p.m.

ART GALLERIES AND EXHIBITION ROOMS

Palace of the Society of the Friends of the Fine Arts, pl. Szczepański 4, tel. 22-66-16

Salon of the Society of the Friends of the Fine Arts, Nowa Huta, al. Róż 3, tel. 44-34-61

Exhibition Hall of the Bureau for Artistic Exhibitions, pl. Szczepański 3A, tel. 22-40-21

"Arkady" Gallery of the Bureau for Artistic Exhibitions, pl. Szczepański 3A, tel. 22-40-21

"Pryzmat" Gallery, ul. Łobzowska 3

Modern Art Gallery, ul. Floriańska 34, tel. 22-74-86

"Krzysztofory" Gallery of the Cracow Group Artistic Association, ul. Szczepańska 2, tel. 22-93-60

Gallery of Cricot 2 Theatre, ul. Kanonicza 5, tel. 22-83-32

Galleries of the Polish Photographic Artists' Union, ul. św. Anny, tel. 22-46-49, and ul. Solskiego 24, tel. 22-24-00

Exhibition Hall of the Cracow Photographic Society, Rynek Główny 17, tel. 22-04-38.

Galleries of the International Press and Book Clubs, Mały Rynek 4, tel. 22-46-60; Nowa Huta, pl. Centralny 1, tel. 44-17-50

"Forum" Gallery of the Community Club, ul. Mikołajska 2, tel. 22-49-00

"Millennium" Gallery of the CPLiA, ul. Stolarska 13

"Propozycje" Gallery of the PAX Association, ul. Garbarska 9

"38" Gallery, Rynek Główny 7, tel. 21-36-72

"Imago-Artis" Gallery of Silverware, ul. Florianska 10, tel. 22-89-36

"Imago-Artis" Gallery of Silver and Gold Ware, ul. Szpitalna 1

"Jaszczury" Photographic Gallery, Rynek Główny 7

Gallery of Marian Gołogórski and Bogusław Rostworowski, ul. Grodzka 58

"Inny Świat" Gallery of Modern Art of Tadeusz Nyczek and Maciej Szybist, ul. Floriańska 37

Gallery of Andrzej Mleczko, ul. św. Jana 19

Gallery of Pure and Applied Art, pl. Szczepański 5

"Pod Złotym Lewkiem" Gallery of Modern Art of Danuta Fróg-Górecka, ul. Szewska 18

"Farbiarnia" Gallery of Jadwiga Szymanowska, ul. Grodzka 2

Black Gallery of Modern Art of Jacek Szmuc. ul. św. Jana 24

"DESA" Gallery (Polish 19th and 20th cent. painting, jewellery and applied art), ul. św. Jana 3, tel. 22-98-91

"Kramy Dominikańskie" Gallery (modern painting, sculpture and applied art), ul. Stolarska 10

Gallery of Artistic Glassware, ul. Stolarska 12

"B"Gallery (drawing, graphic art, jewellery, exotic art), ul. Solskiego 21, tel. 22-93-82

Art Gallery of the National Publishing Agency, ul. Floriańska 33

Art Gallery (Polish painting, jewellery, glassware, earthenware, furniture), Nowa Huta, os. Ogrodowe 10. tel. 44-33-90

Maria Anna Potocka's Gallery — DESA Museum of Current Art (modern painting and sculpture), pl. gen. Sikorskiego 10 (in the courtyard)

THEATRES

Juliusz Słowacki Theatre, pl. św. Ducha 1, tel. 22-45-75

Miniature Theatre, pl. św. Ducha 1, tel. 22-45-75

Stary Theatre named after Helena Modrzejewska, pl. Szczepański 1, tel. 22-85-66

Kameralny Theatre, ul. Bohaterów Stalingradu 21, tel. 21-19-98

Cellar at Sławkowska (Stary Theatre), ul. Sławkowska 14, tel. 22-85-66

Bagatela Theatre named after Tadeusz Boy-Żeleński, ul. Karmelicka 6, tel. 22-45-44

Ludowy Theatre, Nowa Huta, os. Teatralne 34, tel. 44-27-66

Groteska Puppet and Mask Theatre, ul. Skarbowa 2, tel. 33-37-62

Cricot 2 Theatre, ul. Kanonicza 5, tel. 22-83-32

STU Theatre, al. Krasińskiego 18, tel. 22-22-63, auditorium in the tent, ul. Rydla 31, tel. 37-42-54

Maszkaron Theatre of Satire, ul. Bohaterów Stalingradu 21 and Rynek Główny, Town Hall Tower, tel. 21-50-16

"38" Theatre, Rynek Główny 7, tel. 21-36-72

Ewa Demarczyk's Theatre, ul. Floriańska 55

Music Theatre of Opera and Operetta, ul. Lubicz 48, tel. 21-22-66 (switchboard), Opera, pl. św. Ducha 1, tel. 22-45-75

Karol Szymanowski Philharmonic Hall, ul. Zwierzyniecka 1, tel. 22-94-77

"Jama Michalikowa" Cabaret, ul. Floriańska 45, tel. 22-15-61

"Piwnica pod Baranami" Cabaret, Rynek Główny 27, tel. 22-18-84

NOTES

NOTES

NOTES

NOTES